Confid
Your Pr
Training

How to Develop Healthy Self Esteem and Deep Self Confidence to Be Successful and Become True Friends with Yourself

Positive Psychology Coaching Series

Copyright © 2016, 2017 by Ian Tuhovsky

Author's blog: www.mindfulnessforsuccess.com

Author's Amazon profile: amazon.com/author/iantuhovsky

Instagram profile:
https://instagram.com/mindfulnessforsuccess

All rights reserved. No part of this publication may be reproduced, stored in a retrieval system, or transmitted, in any form or by any means, electronic, mechanical, photocopying, recording or otherwise without the prior written permission of the author and the publishers.

The scanning, uploading, and distribution of this book via the Internet, or via any other means, without the permission of the author is illegal and punishable by law.

Please purchase only authorized electronic editions, and do not participate in or encourage electronic piracy of copyrighted materials.

Important

The book is not intended to provide medical advice or to take the place of medical advice and treatment from your personal physician. Readers are advised to consult their own doctors or other qualified health professionals regarding the treatment of medical conditions. The author shall not be held liable or responsible for any misunderstanding or misuse of the information contained in this book. The information is not indeed to diagnose, treat or cure any disease.

It's important to remember that the author of this book is not a doctor/therapist/medical professional. Only opinions based upon his own personal experiences or research are cited. The author does not offer medical advice or prescribe any treatments. For any health or medical issues – you should be talking to your doctor first.

Please be aware that every e-book and "short read" I publish is written truly by me, with thoroughly researched content 100% of the time. Unfortunately, there's a huge number of low quality, cheaply outsourced spam titles on the Kindle non-fiction market these days, created by various internet marketing companies. **I don't tolerate these books. I want to provide you with high quality, so if you think that one of my books/short reads can be improved in any way, please contact me at:**

contact@mindfulnessforsuccess.com

I will be very happy to hear from you, because that's who I write my books for!

TABLE OF CONTENTS:

PART I: INTRODUCTION—The Social Layer 6
Preface: Self-confidence and self-esteem vs. social conditioning 6

PART II: SELF-CONFIDENCE 39
Being natural 39
What does self-confidence really boil down to? 46
Reach out and touch self-confidence 55
What self-confidence is and what it is not 62
Self-confidence as an emotion................................ 66
The overprotective mind and useless fear 68
What to do to develop your self-confidence every day 93
Facing the fear 97
EVERYTHING is a stressor.................................... 106
How to be self-confident when "nothing works" 115
Your relation with yourself 123
Getting out of your comfort zone 132
How to be self-confident in professional relations 136
A few more important words about self-confidence and the proper mindset 141

PART III: SELF-ESTEEM 153
The "recipe for self-esteem"................................. 157
Six pillars of healthy self-esteem 161
Mindfulness and awareness—the first two steps to real and healthy self-esteem 182
The social context 194
The extraordinary relation between self-acceptance and stress 209
The enormous importance of self-support............ 214

How to protect your self-esteem when life brings you down 220

How to deal with jealousy...229

Stop pretending and begging for acceptance!........................237

Make your own "value box" 249

One step at a time..251

PART IV: Practical exercises and NLP tools 258
Guidelines 262

Facing your inner personalities...263

Changing your personal history 271

Rebirth 277

The pattern of giving yourself true love 282

Perceptual positions 287

Dealing with criticism...292

Stop dwelling on bad memories 295

Self-confidence anchor 297

Projection of resources into the future 307

Reframing the most difficult situations 312

Swoosh..316

Expectation-related pressure relief 318

Daily affirmations and goals (short term).............................321

Present-moment awareness...323

Mirror training 327

Outro 330
My Free Gift to You – Get One of My Audiobooks For Free! 343

Recommended Reading for You 346
About The Author...356

PART I: INTRODUCTION—The Social Layer

Preface: Self-confidence and self-esteem vs. social conditioning

These are interesting times we live in. While more and more people become socially awkward and seem to be offended by just about anything, there's another group that seems to be living their lives almost exclusively through social media, becoming more and more narcissistic, with their smartphones practically glued to their hands and faces. Constantly worried about their social perception and about maintaining their (oftentimes fake) image, they lose contact with their true selves. All of this is seriously out of balance and also scary, in a way. Both of these increasingly popular phenomena show that healthy self-esteem and natural self-confidence are rare commodities in our Western societies.

Apart from the above trends, there is a vast "average" layer. These are people who often feel socially anxious, people who are shy, insecure and doubtful about things, about themselves, about their own way.

There are also people who live "normal lives" and appear to be "just fine," but due to their problems with self-esteem and self-confidence often stumble over obstacles they should never be stumbling over. None of those behavioral patterns have anything to do with healthy self-esteem.

The first thing many people say about themselves is that they are insufficient. It's a little bit more difficult for most to admit that they are magnificent, but considering the vast number of narcissistic and self-obsessed personalities these days, it's also quite common. The healthy way between these extremes is the rarest, mostly because people are lacking in objective self-esteem and self-awareness.

Lack of self-confidence and problems with unhealthy self-esteem are usually the reason why smart, competent and talented people never achieve a satisfying life, a life that should easily be possible for them.

Now, I'm not saying that I have all the answers and I'm the one who dictates the wrong and the right way to go through your own life. But since you've probably been looking for valuable knowledge about confidence, just ask yourself if the way you live now is the way you want to spend the rest of your life. Do you like what you do? Is it a result of your own decision, or of what others told you to do? Do you truly feel good in your own skin? Do you feel safe about your position? Do you feel good with where you are in your life? Do you feel free from the shackles of your own mind and the chains of the society? Do you often feel judged? Do you feel socially comfortable? Are you building your self-esteem on solid foundations, or are you perhaps building it on quicksand?

If you are looking for self-confidence and self-esteem-oriented books, you probably already know that there's something you should change about your life. Congratulations—you've found the right one.

This is basically a **"if I did it, so can you" type of story**. I myself used to be a shy guy with many demons inside of his head; I used to be that uncomfortable fellow on trembling legs whose awkward vibe made everyone else in the room feel upset as well. I often obsessed about what other people might or might not think about me. Sometimes, I was seriously laughed at, for a number of reasons. At two points of my life, I felt so bad and down I needed the help of a psychotherapist. I'm still a young person, but for some reason I've gone through a lot of harshness during my life. It wouldn't be arrogant to say I've probably gone through more than some 50-year-old people. The many serious bumps, sharp turns and collisions of my life and the ways I managed to overcome them have taught me a lot, and hopefully I will now be able to give you a helping hand.

Thanks to the mindset and techniques I'm going to tell you about in this book, I'm barely the same man I used to be, even though **I never changed WHO I really was**. I just changed **HOW I was**. I changed my mindset and my approach to life.

As a kid, I would hide under the table every time my parents or my nanny invited anyone home and there was no way to coax me out. I would often behave like a scared little puppy—it's embarrassing, but true. I used to be extremely shy, that's for sure. During the first 18 years of my life, I was often very awkward in social situations. I was petrified anytime I needed to ask an older person anything or turn to them directly, and I was often afraid of being left alone or abandoned. I often felt terribly anxious and I didn't know the reason why. I also didn't like the way I looked and I had a hard time accepting myself.

On the other hand, I wasn't in the worst position possible. I've always had good friends. People always liked me and somehow I never became a scapegoat. I even had my own personal bodyguards at school—big, strong guys who thought I was funny. Also, girls always liked me—although because I was too shy, and because no man ever had handed me an "instruction manual to the feminine mind and how not to be a muff" when I needed it, interactions with girls usually ended in me making a terrible bum of myself. Taking all this into consideration, there was **a lot** to be done, and so... I eventually did take care of these things.

I can say I successfully transformed myself—even though I still often hate talking to people on the phone, especially in foreign languages.

I'm not a demon of confidence, and as opposed to what personality tests show, I generally consider myself an introvert—but the progress I have made is astounding. I overcame all of my social fears, like talking to strangers at meetings or on the streets, dating beautiful and smart women, traveling alone to other countries and continents and networking and making new friends. I learned how to inspire and intrigue people with what I had to say. I learned how to give public speeches. I overcame many of my insecurities related to the fact that I'm a small and skinny guy. I managed to quit the job I despised and started my own business. I learned how to stop being jealous and feeling inferior to others. I destroyed the need to prove myself to others and the need for show-off behaviors. I overcame my extreme fear of heights.

I learned how to defend myself verbally and how to take things in stride... and the list goes on.

I know the Internet is FULL of these "success" stories, oftentimes fake, so you might think I'm just another "rags to riches" type of guy with a beautiful Hollywood-like background story, as unreal as it is appealing.

But no, I'm not a guru. I'm not even a guy who overcame ALL of his adversities. **There's no such thing in real life and it's extremely important that you comprehend this.** It's like in the REM song, "Everybody Hurts." Everyone who claims to be "that guy" who "has it all already figured out" **is nothing but just another liar.** I know because I have met quite a lot of famous people, coaches, "gurus" and so on. They all have their problems, despite the successes they have had. The truth is life kicks everyone's ass and there's no such thing as an eternal sweet spot. **Unfortunately, not many people interested in self-development want to hear this.** People want shortcuts and so the marketers take advantage and sell these impossible dreams to people.

I'm not a guy with a backstory along the lines of "I used to be dead-broke, all alone, fat, ugly, with no teeth and stupid, but today I'm a millionaire; I own fifty businesses, none of which I have to care about at all; I met and married the best woman on this planet; I have no fear; I feel no anger, pain or hunger. In fact, I'm so cool I will never die. Additionally, I cured my third-stage cancer with affirmations and occasionally I'm able to levitate and shine with colorful auras. Just buy my $699 course to find out how!"

I'm just a "hometown boy makes good" type of person who **believes in good karma and providing value,** and I'm going to show you the solutions that have worked for me and my friends. Some of them are "quick fixes" that can help you a ton and relatively quickly. Some are not, though, and will require a strong will and some time and effort put into them.

Any change in life requires perseverance, so if you're looking for a **"magic pill"** for all of your problems, you might as well grab another 25-page Kindle spam pamphlet from the first page of Amazon search, titled "Confidence: Confidence: The Ultimate Confidence Solution for Self-Confidence and Self-Esteem Confidence" authored by a "coach" with a beautiful iStock photo, who also happens to have published pamphlets about Miley Cyrus, the paleo diet, the stock market, bio gardening and the ultimate diarrhea cure. To help you even more, this book should also be edited by "Confidence," with photographs taken by "Self-Esteem."

Rant off for now, but the reality is still on. **My books are not outsourced content just published for a quick buck and thus will require real <u>action</u> taken by you!** This is not a comfort-fast-food for the mind.

Magic pills don't exist, period. Many times in this book I will ask you to write down different details and your insights. **So, here's your first homework:** go and buy a notebook in which you will be doing all the exercises from this book. This notebook will be a witness to your success. It will be your confidence notebook.

So, having said all that—are you ready? Let's get this party started!

Your Free Mindfulness E-book

I really appreciate the fact that you took an interest in my work!

I also think it's great you are into self-development and proactively making your life better.

This is why I would love to offer you a free, complimentary 120-page e-book.

It's about Mindfulness-Based Stress and Anxiety Management Techniques.

It will provide you with a solid foundation to kick-start your self-development success and help you become much more relaxed, but at the same time, more focused and effective person. All explained in plain English, and it's a useful free supplement to this book.

To download your e-book, please visit:

http://www.tinyurl.com/mindfulnessgift

Enjoy!
Thanks again for being my reader! It means a lot to me!

Face the truth

In today's world of "political correctness," everyone is told to be a "special, little beautiful snowflake," but in the **real** world, it doesn't matter. Why? Simply because **no one really gives a damn.** There's a social narrative telling us that we all **deserve** this and that, but here comes the harsh reality: **we don't deserve anything**, simply meaning that we **can't expect** anyone or anything to **give us anything**, just because we wish so or would like life to be like that. That's how this world has been operating since forever, since billions of years ago, way before mankind had even appeared on this beautiful blue planet to have invented human rights, the Constitution, sliced bread, biochemical weapons of mass destruction and pants. It's called the survival of the fittest. Some people might feel "offended" by that. That's good, as it just proves my point.

If you are confident and have healthy self-esteem, you just can't be bothered to feel "offended" every few days. In fact, making a truly confident person feel offended by almost anything at all is close to impossible. The reason all these people feel "offended" nowadays is mainly that they look at themselves and at life the wrong way—their sense of being offended is self-imposed. They give other people and events **permission** to offend them. You can't feel bad about anyone saying anything negative unless that's what **you** really think of yourself. If you are self-confident, you don't obsess over how other people perceive you. You are not overly concerned about your image. That doesn't mean that you should be cool with being homeless and having a flea farm on your dirty head, but you might just not feel the need to update your social media statuses every hour and share every day of your life on the Internet with the two thousands "friends" of yours, who usually don't even give a crap about your life and wouldn't spend a dime or a minute of their time **if you truly needed help.**

If you want to change anything serious in your life, you have to FACE the truth. **You are on your own.** The government and the politicians won't save you. The majority of them don't care about you, in any given country on this planet. They've all been professionally taught how to lie to people since even before they got into real politics, no matter whether they say they believe in God or not. Your parents won't save you and won't do your work for you. At some point, your friends will start their own families and businesses, will start making careers or go abroad and part ways with you… and they won't help you, either. No one will do what has to be done for you. In fact, we don't even deserve such fundamental rights as **equal treatment under the law**, because after all, **if we don't fight for it, we don't get it.** Sad, but true. In fact, it's only sad if you consider it to be. It's neither good nor bad; it is how it is. The system and the shape of things haven't changed much since prehistory and Paleolithic times. The strongest wins.

I would like 25-year-old bourbon to start flowing from my kitchen tap and also a guaranteed bestseller spot for every single book I publish, but my wishful thinking doesn't change much. We, the small ones, have to adapt to the universal laws, not the other way around.

The reason that some minorities are stronger than others in the US and many other countries these days is that they got their crap together and **fought for it. They said, "Enough with the sickness!"** They started rioting, started getting good education, started organizing themselves in strong and well-managed groups, and started standing up for their rights much more often. Then they began developing their own businesses and social movements. They also started making careers in media, law and politics. **Instead of just wishfully expecting, they went for it**. They stopped being passive. Now you can often see these social minorities playing leading roles in the law, the government, the media, and so on.

The same goes to your confidence and self-esteem. You can't just sit back and expect to magically start feeling good; you can't expect other people to start treating you like they treat all these truly confident people. You can't expect your life to change **at all if** you remain passive. It's about facing reality. **It's about being active. I once heard this bold thought from my friend's dad:** "The world doesn't care about your self-esteem. The world will expect you to accomplish something BEFORE you feel good about yourself."

The miracle of "self"

At the same time though, you **are** a miracle, indeed. Why? Think about it this way: your genealogical tree is at least a few millions years old. Every single relationship and every single generation in these countless past years had led to your parents finally meeting each other. One of the millions of spermatozoids reached that one ovum, creating a new life. I don't know if there are numbers known to humankind that are big enough to even estimate how big a coincidence it was and how lucky you are to be alive on this planet. From the perspective of statistics and biology, you truly are a miracle.

Who you now are is a consequence of the past—the past before you were even born, and the past since your birth. Everything you've gone through, every single moment you have survived constitutes your character, your uniqueness, your "self." All these things made you the very person you are right now. Do you know why this is important? **It's important because, among many other things, real and unshakable self-confidence and self-esteem come from realizing your own uniqueness.** They come from finally noticing how special you are.

We have all heard our entire lives that we should be something else in order to finally reach happiness—that we are not enough, that we should be different, that we should change, that we need to own this or that, that we should become a doctor, CEO, professor or lawyer, build a big house and plant a tree, become a father or a mother, go to this or that university or college; that we are not suitable for this or that, that we should never say or think certain things, and so on. During the long and often bothersome education and socialization stage, in kindergarten, school and college we so frequently hear, "Change yourself! Change yourself!" All of this leads to a low level of self-esteem. All the things that other people keep repeating and telling us—"Can't do this; shouldn't do that; that's improper!"—in our lives, especially during the childhood and teenage years, we take as our own. **We take them for granted and rarely question them.** Meanwhile, in reality, you don't usually have to be perceived well by others, and certainly not by everyone. However, you do have to perceive yourself well. **It's your job.** Life's too short to be insecure. Life's too short not to be your own fan.

Suppose at some stage of your life you decide to go to a seminar where you've been told that some guru-experts can magically change your life in a matter of hours, if only you pay them a certain amount of money (probably your last month's paycheck). You go there and what do you hear? *Change yourself! Change yourself! Change yourself! I know better what's good for you! To be self-confident, you need to act like James Bond and move like a real gangster! You need to have these, and not those clothes! So you say you are a vulnerable painter, not a killer? How bad! You can't speak like that; this is wrong! Only think as long as you need to and not even a single moment longer, because after this moment, there's a doubt lurking!* And so it goes. Go past that bullshit: self-confidence and self-esteem are not about becoming someone else. They're not about changing who you are! Don't change yourself.

Change your bad habits, change your thought-patterns, change your environment, change your friends if you have to, change your detrimental behaviors, even change your beliefs if they are **not helpful** in your life, but stay who you are. Be true to your real essence, your real soul. Evolve; develop yourself; but don't change your true self. If you do anything to become somebody else, it's the worst thing you could possibly do. That's how the term "self-confidence" came about. It's about being confident in your SELF. **YOUR** self, not someone else's self! It's about knowing both your **strong and weak sides**, your attributes, if you will, being aware and consciously using your uniqueness to succeed, while being at peace with your nature.

Confidence means that you feel good about yourself in almost every situation and that your self-esteem is healthy. When you are self-confident and your level of self-awareness is high, you know who you are and how you are, and other people's words and opinions can hardly affect the way you feel.

But it also works the other way around! If you only feed yourself with cajolery and fantastic opinions about yourself, becoming stuck in your "safe-space," where no bad opinion about you can ever reach your ears or eyes, avoiding all the harshness of reality, you are much easier to hurt and offend. You become weak and soft like an undercooked muffin. Why? Because you have built your ego on a foundation of other people's positive opinions. A truly self-confident person doesn't look for acceptance, doesn't need to constantly prove their value to others, looking into their eyes to see any sign of approval, like a small puppy or a kitten waiting for a permission before it will start eating.

Self-confident people don't need fancy cars, new gadgets or houses that could fit 20 entire families inside to feel good about themselves. They don't need to feel worried because they aren't "lumbersexual," or because they are "lumbersexual" but on TV they just said it stopped being fashionable and trendy roughly six days ago, and now they should maybe start shaving their eyebrows to be manly, or feminine, or cool, or modern, according to society.

Explore yourself, discover yourself and then DEVELOP yourself and evolve, staying yourself at the same time. The more you KNOW yourself, the more you know who you are, the more self-aware you become and the more SELF-confident you can be, isn't it obvious? Looking at the society we live in, apparently not! If you are not honest, not at peace with your true self and your inner nature, if you want to be something else, then you **can't** be self-confident by definition. Maybe you can be **non-self**-confident then; **confident in the fake character you have created**, but it's a losing game.

Does this mean that, for example, if you're a fucking lazy ass and you don't feel like doing anything at all but watching TV and eating junk food, you should stay that way because that's your true self? Hell NO! Laziness is just an escape from getting in touch with your true self and realizing yourself, an escape from using the SELF in everyday life. When you are truly SELF-confident, then you should want to do everything to **make the most of yourself in life**. It all could be phrased in the words of Reinhold Niebuhr: "God, grant me the serenity to accept the things I cannot change, the courage to change the things I can, and the wisdom to know the difference." Are you confident, or do you want to be confident? Either way, take good care of yourself. Respect yourself! If you want to feel your value, then value yourself, your decisions and actions. Be honest; be real. Keep your own word to yourself. The mission is to become your own best friend. You have to treat yourself as one. Self-confident people don't laugh at jokes that aren't funny to them, don't go to places they don't really want to go. They act in accordance with their own values.

They are not perfect; they are **aware** of that, and they **don't even want** to be perfect, as such a thing **doesn't exist** if you're a human being. Though, if you are a supreme, extra-intelligent, astral being from another galaxy, then I'm glad you found a minute to read my humble book.

Be perfect in your own way; that's what really beautiful. Self-confident people create their own environment, an environment where they can be themselves, instead of trying to fit into other people's lives. You can have authorities and role models, but don't idolize them. They are just humans. Using your favorite heroes or inspirational people as encouragements and examples for personal growth is one thing; comparing yourself to those you perceive as "lesser" or "better" than you is a death sentence for your advancement in your personal self-improvement. When thinking negatively about and tearing others down by comparing or judging them in my head, I was basically just wasting my energy, energy that I could have been investing in myself. This is time I could have been redirecting and investing into positively building myself up.

There will always be someone better or worse at something than you, and comparing will be a trap that is impossible to escape. Besides—what does it matter if someone is better or worse than you? Wouldn't you like to be confident and successful on your own terms? When we are independently secure within ourselves, we open our minds to see the gifts that others can provide, without expectation but with extreme gratitude.

Illusions and smokescreens

Before going deeply into the topic of self-confidence and self-esteem, let's pierce through the social surface layer. So often society makes us look up to celebrities, pop stars, famous writers, models, spiritual gurus and even politicians. We intuitively feel that what we are shown in the media (famous people in expensive cars, houses reminiscent of palaces, beautiful and perfect bodies and big crowds loving them) are not the real lives these people live. In my early teenage years, I played electric guitar in a rock band and I badly wanted to become a rock star. I really thought their lives were so much superior to mine—big concerts with thousands of people shouting how they loved the band, bunches of beautiful girls wanting to spend nights with them, countless hours of fun in the recording studios and the ability to tell people exactly what they felt and earn millions of dollars in return.

After some time passed, though, I started wondering why so many of these rock and roll bands were disintegrating; why almost every week we hear about Hollywood stars going to rehab, undergoing countless divorces, driving under the influence, going crazy or committing suicide. Slowly, I started seeing things how they really were. After having read many different rock, rap and movie stars' biographies and interviews, I saw the real world so many of them were living in: constant pressure to stay at the top; extremely exhausting concert tours; rehearsing the same songs for years and years; psycho-fans, stalkers and haters; drug and alcohol addictions; wrecked mental and physical health due to a total lack of life balance; destroyed relationships with family, friends or children; jealousy, divorces, detachment from reality, narcissism, depression, heavy lawsuits, arguments with management and record companies and many other not-so-sweet things.

Of course, there are many famous rock bands, actors and other artists with normal and happy lives, but my point here is the reason we struggle with insecurity is because **we compare our behind-the-scenes with everyone else's highlight reel**.

Believe me, Angelina Jolie, Johnny Depp and Eminem also have to go to the bathroom twice a day and "take the poo to the loo." Famous people also eat and urinate; they have nightmares at night and bad breath in the morning. They vomit when they drink too much; they have mental breakdowns, bad relationships, and nasty spots on their faces; they feel stressed and pressured and some days they don't feel any reason to even get out of bed. They are just mortal human beings, but due to the brainwashing the media and the Internet serve us every day, **we so often seem to simply forget about this obvious fact, even if it's "just" on a subconscious level.** We look at our friends posting happy pictures on Facebook and Instagram and we feel that our own lives are miserable compared to theirs. People are constantly looking for a reference; they want to see how their lives look in comparison to other people's. You need to quit this losing game. It will lead you astray. **You can and you should be inspired by other people**, but don't try to copy their world or try match them. Instead of being the next best thing, be the best of your own kind. You don't have to walk the paths that other people have shown you.

Compare your life to your own life from a month, two months or five months ago. Compare it to the vision of the life you have designed for yourself to find some motivation and get a kick in the butt, but don't compare it to the fake and selected images people show you on social media or during all the chit-chats you have with them. Most people are just attention-seekers; they always do things to make other people feel jealous. Notice that a man will never post a picture on Facebook of himself crying into a pillow for two hours because his cat died and the girl he had a crazy crush on chose his friend over him. They would rather post a picture of their new car (or their dad's car) to make themselves feel good. No girl will ever post a picture of herself eating two buckets of ice cream, sitting under a blanket in an old, sweaty and stretched tracksuit, blowing her nose on toilet paper, next to the mirror she just broke with a furious kick because she thought she was too fat or too skinny or her nose looked bad. She would rather post a selfie with her best friends and lots of cleavage to gain 400 "likes" and make herself feel good about her appearance.

Remember: don't compare your real life to the illusions other people and the media are constantly creating for you!

Indicators of weakness

While I'm on that topic, have you ever noticed how often a show of strength is nothing but an indicator of weakness? I think we all know people who do everything all the time to appear successful to others. I personally remember a few people (who I don't hang around anymore), whose income I would describe as good (usually triple the national average), but who roll like oil kings or ghetto gangsters—they drive cars they can't afford, always have the newest smartphones and gadgets, wear fancy and expensive clothes, live in big show-off houses and generally do everything possible to fulfill their deep and fiery desire to be respected and to show other people that their lives are superior and they are doing better. They do it all to maintain the fake image of themselves they have created.

The funny thing is, the REALLY successful and smart people of this world usually look and act normal. Go ahead and take a look at Mark Zuckerberg, the creator, owner and CEO of Facebook, one of the richest and most powerful people on this planet. He usually wears a gray hoodie, inconspicuous sport shoes and a pair of jeans. He doesn't create the image of an almighty, fearsome billionaire or gangster. If someone from a hypothetical country where they don't have any media or the Internet saw him, they would think he was just a normal, middle-class guy. Steve Jobs? He usually wore a black turtleneck, white sport shoes and old jeans. I can't remember him wearing a $50,000 Rolex, five grand snake-leather shoes and a ten grand tailor-made suit. He drove an old Mercedes SL, which is a nice and not-so-cheap sports car, but nothing extremely fancy or exorbitantly expensive. Ingvar Kamprad, the founder and owner of IKEA, also one of the richest men of the world, dresses like an average grandpa, drives an old Volvo and is said to still live in his old apartment in an old block tower. If you take a look at many billionaires and multimillionaires of this world, you will see that many of them don't live lavish show-off lives to impress other people. They DON'T HAVE TO. I'm not saying that these people never use their money to live big—most of them own their own Pacific islands, seaside villas or private jet planes, but it's not their primary focus or something they want so badly to show to others. They don't have to prove themselves to media or fans. Isn't it funny that an average *nouveau riche* looks and acts like someone at first sight richer than, for example, Mark Zuckerberg? That's what happens when people with unstable self-confidence or low self-esteem become successful. It results in an overwhelming and persistent need to show others how big and great they are, even if they are just slightly more successful than other people. The conclusion here is that often enough, the more some people parade and live a show-off lifestyle, the more it indicates internal problems they have with themselves. Sometimes such things as money, physical strength, and status can show people's weaknesses. Notice how some big guys at gyms act normally, just doing their thing, while others spend lots of time posing in front of mirrors, making irritating noises while throwing dumbbells and barbells, shouting and bragging to others how cool they are or constantly commenting on girls they've had or fights they were in. Guess who's probably really insecure about themselves in this picture. The same is usually true with people always desperately trying to be the center of attention at parties, school bullies, guys acting aggressively and going "gangsta" in clubs, or girls who go there half-naked, sexually dancing like crazy in the middle of the dance floor and other well-lit areas, shouting like little kids and taking selfies every three seconds, while constantly acting arrogantly and extremely rude towards other people. Think about Instagram attention-seekers, etc.

As a general rule, almost every exaggerated and oft-repeated behavior is pointing to low confidence and internal fears, such as fear of being weak, ignored, unnoticed by other people, poor, etc. The people who really feel insecure are often the ones who act show-offish and want so badly to prove to others how very extraordinarily confident they are.

Rejections and equality

I have also noticed that quite often people who have very high status and are wealthy, good-looking and well-dressed have big problems meeting new people, acting naturally at parties, dating, forming intimate relationships, etc. I have a few friends who earn tons of money, look better than most Hollywood actors and models, are CEOs of respectable companies and generally live seemingly successful lives, but have big trouble meeting interesting women and forming healthy relationships—mostly because they are afraid to even start meeting new people. **Why?** They think that because of all they have achieved they shouldn't be treated like other people, but better—that they should never be ignored or laughed at and all the people they meet should respect them because of what they have become. Unfortunately for them, that's not how this world works. Imagine a hypothetical situation in which Jonny Depp or Ewan

McGregor approaches a random girl on your town's streets and asks her for a phone number. He expects her to jump out of her shoes and probably faint, but instead gets a rude answer and no phone number in return. By the way, yes, that's entirely possible—one of my female friends flaked on Larry Mullen, Jr. from U2 in one of Dublin's pubs, just because he was drunk and smelled like buzz, and she had a terrible hangover and a crazy headache, was on her period and never really liked U2 anyway. Don't you think our celebrity would be totally shocked and crushed for a good few hours afterwards? A small-town girl just ignored an international movie or music star, a handsome devil and a popular millionaire loved by crowds. He would probably suffer more and feel much worse than a "regular Joe" working at Walmart would in the same situation with the same woman. Often enough, that's a natural psychological mechanism that kicks in when someone with low or usual self-esteem achieves quick success, or just never really works on their fear of rejection. It can be easily taken care of when someone decides to learn how to achieve and maintain natural self-confidence and healthy self-esteem. Anyway, that's definitely something you need to think about.

The system

Speaking of illusions, do you know the reason the media, politicians and big companies want us to feel insufficient all the time? It's because a human being who feels complete and fulfilled won't need a new car every six months, won't need another useless phone gadget to impress other people, won't need to watch another six seasons of a sad TV series or go on a crazy shopping spree to make themselves feel better. The reason we are kept that way, the reason we are constantly shown all these "perfect" bodies and happy faces and are told, "You need this, you need that, you want this and you certainly crave those" is to **make us good, passive consumers.** And no, **this is not a conspiracy theory.** If you ask me how I know— I'm a sociologist, that was one of my specializations in school and I've been into these topics for a long time now. But if you don't want to take my word for granted, then just ask anyone deep enough into Internet or media marketing and "content creation." They will tell you the same thing with a little help from a good scotch on the table. Practically **everything we experience in the social arena** is intended and aimed exclusively to turn us into dumb sheep and good consumers, as are the news, social narratives, popular social and oftentimes even religious values, education the way it currently is and even things like marriages and diamond engagement rings. Google this: "story behind diamond engagement." Yes, it was just a very successful brainwashing inflicted on people in the form of a marketing campaign. No romantic story involved. Society wants you to "be normal," so you keep it going and keep feeding the system.

Just go to your job where you usually make tons of money—but for someone else—leave after eight or ten hours, exhausted and dumb like a zombie, get your nice take-out fast(crap)food meal, Starbucks coffee, microwaveable frozen pizza and a beer, go home, watch brainwashing TV or silly cats on the Internet and then go to sleep. Then, after five or six days of repeating this funny loop, when the weekend comes, take your credit card and go shopping-crazy. Buy yourself all the things you don't really need so we can have your money and you can feel better about yourself. And then post your pictures on social media to show others how happy you are. Or, if you can't take this dullness anymore, visit your shrink and take another dose of anti-depressants. And, of course, they... cost you money. Side effects of long-term use? No such thing! Come on! Be "normal"!

That's how the system works. Self-aware and awakened people wouldn't want to be like someone else, wouldn't need all these materialistic things to feel better, wouldn't watch most of the extremely dumb, low-quality TV shows, follow the lives of celebrities or listen to the poor muzak on the radio.

Notice how the majority of radio and TV mainstream "music" consists of silly, naive and simplistic lyrics about "perfect lives" full of free sex, booze and partying "in da club with homies," or about an idealistic, romantic and childish vision of love. The musical layers usually consist of three notes or chords and an extremely simple rhythm repeated for three or four minutes straight. Have you ever felt that all of these "songs" are all the same? Can you even compare them to the goodness of the older music, Pink Floyd or The Smiths, for instance, when it comes to the complexity of the musical layers or intelligence of the lyrics? No, you usually can't. Did you know that 90% of the popular hits on the radio and TV are written and produced by FOUR people? Yes, the majority of these popular idols are just trying to play and recreate (emphasis on "trying," as often their live performances suck hard) what was written by one of the four "hit-makers." Real artists usually write their own music and lyrics. The vast majority of this fast-food muzak is just a cog in the big business, rarely an art.

You might not know this, but popular music often puts you in a trance, especially when you are tired and driving your car. And what comes next? Yeah, commercials, telling you to buy things. Or news, telling you that this world is a dangerous, scary and gloomy place and that the politicians and big businesses will protect you and gently hold your hand.

And you usually listen to all this in a state of no awareness and very low consciousness. That's how our subconscious gets accessed easily through the backdoor. That's nothing but a form of hypnosis and that's how we become hardwired. The system would die and economies would start collapsing, slowing down or transforming if people were awakened, self-aware, self-fulfilled and conscious enough—if they were just too happy with themselves, with nature, with simple interactions with other people and animals, with enjoying their passions and hobbies, minding their own business and that of their local communities. The system always wants to maintain the status quo, no matter what the price is.

Now, as someone born and raised in Eastern Europe, who knows the rotten fruits of real socialism and communism quite well, and as someone too old to be a hippie, I'm definitely **not saying** that capitalism is a bad thing and that we should destroy all the big corporations and live under the trees. **But** these are the things you need to be aware of if you want to free yourself from the shackles of self-doubt, depression and low self-confidence. **It all starts from awareness and, especially, from self-awareness.**

I guess that will be enough for a proper introduction. Let's now cover what self-confidence really is in more detail and learn how to build and nourish it!

PART II: SELF-CONFIDENCE

Being natural

At the beginning, we should talk about what self-confidence really is and how it's being misinterpreted, which makes people wear fake masks.

Many times I have worked with people who suffered from a lack of satisfying intimate relationships, usually coming from their inability to freely meet new people and openly express their emotions or their fear of the opposite sex, for many different reasons. These people, at some point, have usually come to the conclusion that they want to change something. And so, for example, they buy a book about body language, thinking that if they start acting in a certain way, the feeling of confidence will all of sudden appear in their everyday lives. These people very often wear masks instead of working on real, deep self-confidence—at some point they usually start acting or maybe even looking like confident people in social contexts. They often start going to the gym, because they have read that self-confident men and women are well built and look like super heroes or goddesses. Sometimes they focus on getting rich, because they think that confident people usually sleep on piles of money, because that's what they have been told, or that's what they have read somewhere or seen on TV. While there's certainly nothing bad about improving one's quality of life in terms of physical wellness or financial abundance, and it can be a great adventure, too, the mistake these people usually make is thinking they can gain lasting, deep self-confidence just by using different body language or by driving a more expensive car.

Yes, these things can surely help to some extent, especially when you are emotionally developed or when you start from the ground level—then you might feel a tangible boost. On the other hand, though, you may start looking and acting like a confident person because of your decision, but if you don't accept and work through all the things that haunt you from the inside—emotions, beliefs, bad habits and detrimental thought patterns—you will still feel a different kind of energy and different set of emotions from what you would really like to feel and **would** feel as someone **truly self-aware** and **deeply confident**. If you just take advantage of the exterior factors instead of focusing on your interior first, you will remain very easy to offend and your self-confidence will be soft and shaky like a milk jelly.

Now, the most important question to ask is, what's **your** definition of self-confidence? What does it really mean to **you**?

I'd like to ask you to stop reading for a moment, take your "confidence notebook" and a pen and write down your definition and your own meaning of self-confidence. Having done this, maybe you will realize that it's associated with your social beliefs (e.g., what your family told you, what your friends told you), maybe you will find out it's what you've been told in school, but anyways—please, take a moment to write it down. Do it now.

When you're done, write down the exact situations in which you don't feel self-confident. What kind of situation or environment must come into existence to make you feel a lack of self-confidence? For example, it could be public appearances and public speeches. Make it precise—what exactly does "I'm scared of public presentations" mean? Speaking for how many people exactly makes you feel overwhelmed? Fifteen, or a hundred and fifty. You can even write out, on a scale of one to ten, how many points you think you currently have and how many more you need to start feeling confident in these situations. For example, write, "When giving public speeches to audiences much larger than 50 people, I evaluate my confidence as 4/10. I will make it 9/10 by the end of this year. Doing this will be a great help to you once you start working on these areas of your life—it will enable you to start tracking your effects and making them tangible. **Take a few minutes to do it now, and keep your notebook at hand; we will be using it in the next chapter.**

The next step, which serves as the absolute foundation for your self-confidence journey, is to write out all of your strong sides—and I mean ALL OF THEM.

Every single good thing you can possibly find about yourself. All the successes you've had, your looks, traits of your character and personality, what other people and your family like about you—don't omit anything. No matter how small and insignificant it may appear to you—include it on your list! Then take a moment to think which of these attributes and traits you could start exposing more, developing and showing to the world.

Lastly, do the opposite thing—write out everything you think is a flaw in yourself. Write down situations from the past you might not be proud of, events that you feel ashamed of, all of the weak sides you have struggled with your entire life. When you're done, take some time to think about which of these things you usually try to run away from. Also, think deeply about which situations cause you to put on your false mask, trying to fool other people into thinking you don't really have these flaws and are someone else.

In the last chapter of this book, in the exercises section, we will be working with these things you now write down, disarming your weaknesses and reinforcing your strengths. Do it now.

I remember that a long time ago, in my school days, I was very afraid of meeting new people—both men and women. I was afraid of new social situations; I never knew what to talk about when trying to make new friends, which often would make me feel very lonely and anxious. Once I sat down and carefully completed the above exercise, I realized I was really afraid of the fact that people would see that I was afraid and scared, not afraid of approaching them as such. It also struck me that for so long I had been doing everything I could to make people think otherwise—that I'm very self-confident and manly like a berserk Viking warrior, killing thousands of enemies in a row (and a dragon, on occasion) with a single strike of the axe. I wanted to keep the false image of a perfectly fine, cool guy so badly, it made me even more stressed out. Obviously I had read many books about body language by then, so I knew the theory, but my lips would still tremble and my hands would get so sweaty I could turn the Sahara Desert into a beautiful garden. So I decided to stop hiding myself beneath the false mask and start showing my cards. I started approaching people and acting naturally—I would usually tell them things like, "Hi. Um… Listen… I don't feel very good today, I've got a terrible headache and I'm a little bit nervous whenever I want to talk to someone I don't know yet, but you really seem to me like an interesting person/fun guy to hang out with and I think I would like to meet you." I really used to tell strangers these things; I was true to the emotions I felt and to who I was at the time.

I wasn't doing this because I had read somewhere that this was a great social technique, I would have lots of friends and all girls would start to love me. Actually, all the self-dev books were stating otherwise. No, I just came to the realization that acting like someone else doesn't work in the long run and I thought, "Fuck that! Let's see what happens when I actually tell people that I'm scared when starting conversations with strangers." The results were shocking—instead of totally awkward reactions and rejections, like I received at times when I tried to act like a superhero on trembling legs, I generally experienced more openness and warmth from other people. They usually smiled and were very nice to me. Still, some people looked at me like I was an extraterrestrial from Mars, because they could still physically feel my stress, but the general outcome was still better. Moreover, I started viewing my flaws and defects as things I could still act in spite of, instead of viewing them as chains constraining me. Also, all the bad emotions started disappearing much faster during conversations with these strange people. And finally, people started looking at me differently; it was at least three times easier for me to start a natural conversation with someone without feeling like a dork after just a few seconds. Of course, I was still afraid every time I started a new conversation, but these emotions stopped being so overwhelming and in turn I started controlling them (i.e., acting apart from them), not the other way around. After admitting my nervousness in front of strangers a couple times, I started being able to interact with strangers without mentioning it, just knowing that it's OK and normal to feel uneasiness. So when I stopped focusing the conversations on how nervous I was (which can get really awkward if you overdo it and mention it too many times), I got even better. Then, after having met lots of new friends, I got rid of the majority of these negative emotions and started acting ten times more confident, fluent and perfectly cool. The next month,

I was able to act normally—cool, calm and collected. I wasn't mentioning my nervousness to anyone, as I had learned how to control it. Then, it passed entirely and meeting new people became as natural as brushing my teeth. As a final result, I don't have problems with talking about my flaws and shortcomings. I'm just a guy, no James Bond. James Bond doesn't exist in real life. Normal people do. How people judge me is up to them, but as it turns out, they often listen to my flaws with nice smiles on their faces and everything is just fine.

What does self-confidence really boil down to?

Let's now discuss the real meaning of self-confidence. As I already explained in the introduction, we commonly call a person self-confident when they feel good in almost every situation and when their levels of self-esteem are high and healthy. Now, while the topic of self-esteem is crucial in building deep and natural self-confidence, it's so broad it needs an entire separate part of the book. Hence, I have divided this book into two main parts: this one you're reading now, about deep self-confidence as such, in the practical context of making your life better; and the next, covering the topic of healthy, natural self-esteem, which is a necessary basis if you want to maintain your deep self-confidence and make it stable. Let's now focus entirely on the topic of self-confidence in this practical context and the mindset that will get us there.

If you take a closer look at the problem of self-confidence, and if you would perhaps like to feel more of it, you will notice that in fact it's **nothing more than a conviction** that you **know how to do something** and a certainty that **you can actually use that skill in a practical situation**, without any significant problems.

The last part—"use that skill in a practical situation"—is very important. If we look at self-confidence through the prism of this definition, it quickly becomes apparent that self-confidence is not monolithic. It consists of many different aspects and it often happens that someone is self-confident in one situation, while being totally insecure in another. The boss of a big company who gives people orders and manages big social structures on a daily basis can be totally confused when it comes to picking a tie that fits his suit, something he never does without the help of his wife. Have you ever known a shy, artistic type of person who's totally awkward in social situations, but a beast on the stage while playing guitar, dancing or even doing stand-up comedy?

A stunt parachute jumper can be terrified of little kids, while a good manager can be self-confident giving orders to other men and being a strong leader, but terrified by the mere thought of dating a stunningly beautiful woman.

This contradiction stems from the fact that you might lack a certain skill in a given area or lack the strong belief that you can make use of that skill in real life. This is good news, because if self-confidence is not monolithic, we can take care of it and strengthen it using the "eat the elephant" method. So how do you eat an elephant? Just take small bites—it makes the task much easier.

So, if you are doubtful about your self-confidence, or you are sure you need to improve it—**begin with identifying the areas of life in which you already are self-confident.** I'm sure there are lots of such areas, especially in professional contexts or in hobbies or sports you like doing. If that's not the case, you can think of the most obvious things like going to the bathroom, taking a shower or brushing your teeth, making yourself a cup of tea or eating a sandwich— notice that hardly anyone does these things unsteadily and doubtfully because almost everyone is well-experienced in them. You probably have lots of experience walking on two feet, or riding a bicycle, or scratching your nose. I don't think you ever say, "Oh, I don't know how to scratch my nose, should I do it like Tony Robbins, or maybe like Arnold Schwarzenegger? Please, guys, just tell me!" You just scratch your damn nose because you are experienced in doing it; it's obvious. But it wouldn't be so obvious to someone who just survived a car accident a few months ago, and they might feel very insecure when eating a dinner with other people. They would have to gain the experience again. When you first tried to ride a bike you were probably afraid and didn't feel confident, but now it's an obvious and natural thing to do, just like breathing. Why? You learned exactly how to do it and it became natural or even subconscious to you. The same goes for all skills—effective communication, emotional intelligence, socializing, dating and cultivating healthy self-esteem, to name a few. They're just skills like any other!

If you look at it that way, you will realize things aren't that bad. Apart from rare cases of severe mental disorders, **it's impossible not to be self-confident in general—there are just some areas you don't feel self-confident in yet.**

Now comes the tough part, the moment when you need lots of self-honesty. You have to take the piece of paper (which hopefully is a part of the confidence notebook you've bought) from the previous chapter, when I asked you to write down all of your weak sides, and frankly, without any witnesses, identify in which areas you feel you lack self-confidence the most.

Don't just sit on the couch and think. If you want to do it properly, take the notebook and a pen and write down all these things, if you didn't do it in the last chapter. Write out all the things you don't feel confident in. **It would be perfect if you did it now!** Remember, the key is to take action on a daily basis, so don't deceive yourself.

When you're finished, take a look at that list and think about where you could start. Which part of the elephant should you bite first? We have two basic strategies here:

-First of all, you can start from something that will earn you a success quickly, something relatively small and easy to do.

-On the other hand, you can choose something that will create the most noticeable change in your life.

So what should you do? If you don't generally feel too confident, I recommend that you choose the first option. It will give you momentum and allow you to gather some initial experiences. The best method is to start with easy victories instead of going off the deep end. Easy-peasy!

It is as if you wanted to move a big and heavy wardrobe alone. You don't need it to move at the speed of a jet plane. You need to shift it slowly, inch by inch, or you will scratch the floor, or make it collapse and hurt you. You need to push it a little bit from different angles and see what the easiest way is.

So, if self-confidence stems from the fact that we have certain skills and we are sure we can use them in reality, now the question comes, **how do we gain skills in the specific area we are working at?** Once you have identified where to start, the best method is to find someone who's good at this particular thing. Initiate contact with this person and try to cooperate (while also giving as much as you can from your side!), observing carefully how they do what you want to do. Remember, the best idea is to choose only one skill/area/aspect at a time.

Why is it so important to observe someone else? Because the majority of the most important and crucial life skills are very hard, or even impossible, to convey in words! Think of swimming, riding a bicycle, dancing, martial arts or public speaking. You can spend hours talking or reading about these things, but it won't improve your skills too much in real life. But if you know someone who can do it, who you can observe and imitate while receiving feedback, it makes the whole process **incomparably faster and easier.**

That's where many forms of academic education, seminars and books fail. It's good to read and listen to these things, but you can never learn certain skills without taking action in real life and practicing.

The best method is still the old method in which there was always a "master" and people who would learn from him, his apprentices. Apprenticing is something you should always be doing. If you don't know anyone who could be your mentor, these days there are no excuses anyway—you can easily find and connect with skilled people from other ends of the planet. Observe their actions, analyze their mindsets, talk and ask smart questions. And now the most important thing: **try to use your new knowledge and skills in practice as soon as possible!** The fact that the first steps and tasks will be small doesn't matter; the fact that your attempts will probably be inept doesn't matter, either—the sooner you start practicing, the greater the chance that you will really learn the new skill and overcome your problem, instead of just hoarding more and more knowledge like most people do. It's a big chance for you! **The vast majority of the population, influenced by the educational system and college, is addicted to getting new knowledge that often doesn't have much to do with reality and practice.** That's why you can easily have an advantage over most people! Taking action will also set you free from tormenting yourself for sitting back and not doing anything to improve your life. **It will remove the sense of stagnation, which kills your good mood and positive outlook.**

So you want to start with simple tasks and things, and when you can manage them well, move on to the more difficult stuff. If you can't move on, it usually means that there's still something more basic to work on, so you gain valuable feedback and then continue to improve on this area, step by step. It's also important to learn from people who you are sure are really good at what you want to learn. So if someone's saying he's rich, or skilled at martial arts, public speaking or meeting and dating men or women, check it out first and see the proof with your own eyes. Many people brag about things, but you don't want to learn from somebody in real life you haven't even checked on at all. The best idea is to choose people who, instead of bragging, just keep silent and do their particular thing masterfully.

As soon as you gain a new skill, apply it as soon as possible in reality, so it becomes another learned and unconscious competence. Use it as soon as possible, so it really gets in your blood. Once that's done, what should you do next?

Go back to the list you have written down in your "confidence notebook" and take care of the next problem! The best part is that solving each new problem gets easier and easier. It's like learning languages—the more languages you know, the easier it is for you to learn a new one.

Another interesting and comforting thought is that if you have deficiencies in self-confidence, and they radiate over many different areas of your life, it doesn't mean you have to handle all of them at once to feel better, because the more problems you solve, the better you will feel in general—**confidence flows from one area of your life to another!**

Introduce this strategy into your life as soon as possible; it will open doors to many new possibilities and ways of living.

Please, do it and start today—because there are too many people with big hearts, honest smiles and great personalities, who never live good lives, simply because they lack self-confidence! Start implementing these actions steps today. And as you do, read on.

Reach out and touch self-confidence

So is it really possible to be self-confident without having confidence included as an inborn trait of one's character? People often think of themselves and others in terms of character, which always seems to be something independent from us, something given and fixed.

Someone's shy, someone else is self-confident; the former person can envy the latter, but they think they "can't change their character anyway." If you still think about yourself in terms of character, then you give yourself very little ability to change. It's really hard to engage in changing something you consider very hard to change, or not prone to any change at all. If you're tempted by the thought of much higher confidence, it's a great idea to quit thinking about yourself as of a **collection of permanent character traits**, and focus on certain **behaviors** instead.

In this approach, your "self-confidence" is a state accompanying a certain behavior and specific events or circumstances. Sometimes you have more of it, other times not so much, depending on the situation you're in. With this approach, you're not a person doomed to being uncertain and you can start pursuing the goal of broadening the range of circumstances in which you normally feel confident.

Just reflect a little bit on your life and think about yourself in the perspective of the last ten or fifteen years. You will see how your self-confidence has changed as time has passed. If you think about it long enough, you will find situations that caused feelings of uncertainty in you in the past, but that today are just everyday routine that you don't even think about. I remember how a long time ago, freshly after receiving my driver's license, I used to feel a clenching in my stomach every time I realized I was about to drive a car alone. I remember all the mental maneuvers I used to perform just to avoid the driving. In Europe, as opposed to the US, it takes many long months and often a few tries to pass the driving license exam; about 98% of cars (apart from those with big engines) have manual transmissions; often there are not traffic lights everywhere and the infrastructure can be extremely complicated in some places, especially in towns that were build a long time before people even started imagining cars.

Roads are often very narrow, especially in mountainous areas or cities with a plethora of tram lines along the main roads, so fresh, inexperienced drivers have to figure everything out on their own after they finally receive their driver's license. I often felt the fear that the consequences of every single error I could make would be irreversible and I was afraid of taking responsibility for myself, my vehicle and other people on the streets.

Today, driving a car is a pleasure and something so trivial and banal I don't give it a thought at all. I just start the engine and drive to my destination. This is one of the circumstances where my self-confidence has grown exponentially.

What was the rocket that boosted my self-confidence in this particular area high into the sky? Think about all the everyday things you do, about places you often visit and the people you know well.

Imagine you are walking around your house, down the familiar street in your neighborhood, when you're alone or surrounded by people you know and like. See the confidence with which you act, how you tie your shoes, walk your dog, pour the water into the kettle or maybe talk with the vendor on the gas station. Most of these things you do unthinkingly, passively, almost automatically. You probably don't think that what you then feel is the mythical "self-confidence," because you're not used to analyzing your behavior in such situations. You are in your comfort zone.

Again, self-confidence is a signal that you're "at home," in a familiar space, or you're doing something you are experienced in and that you can do well. You are in the safe zone. In the very moment you are leaving the zone, when you are taking a step into the unknown, that's exactly when uncertainty appears. You don't know what awaits you; you don't know how your actions will end.

Years ago I was leaving my comfort zone when I was sitting in the driver's seat and starting the engine. I was entering the unknown, even though I had spent many hours driving with the instructor beforehand. But still, the feeling of uncertainty was fully justified in this case. **Uncertainty is completely appropriate when you're inexperienced at something.**

Confidence is assigned to those areas that are "yours," the areas you know well or have mastered in a way.

Leaving this comfort zone always triggers doubts, uncertainty and even fear. But the more often you do something, or go somewhere, the more experiences connected to this situation you gather, and the more familiar with it you become. The more you own this situation and this sphere, the more you become self-confident, and it has absolutely nothing to do with your character or inborn traits.

Now comes the hard part: the road to self-confidence leads through the experience of uncertainty and facing this uncertainty, again and again, until the uncertainty disappears completely. Either you are willing to accept this and get through some discomfort for a while, or you will remain stuck.

That's what I did with my lack of self-confidence while driving—I would drive and drive and then drive even more, until one day I found it was as natural as walking or brushing my teeth. That's exactly how I overcame my fear of heights as well, to the level of being able to go parasailing or climb high structures with no protection. I started climbing small trees, then going higher and higher, until, after a few years, my fear of heights disappeared almost completely and stopped at the level of common sense and reason (or maybe slightly beyond it...).

The same goes for meeting strange people, making public appearances, going to the gym as a skinny guy, speaking and writing in English and all the other experiences for which the feeling of self-confidence wasn't inborn in me.

Why do people fail in becoming more self-confident? After all, the recipe for self-confidence seems to be fairly easy—start in one area; explore, learn, exercise and experience until you feel confident in that area. Then reach for the next one. And the next one. And so on. The more areas of self-confidence you cover, the more confident a person you become. So now we come to an important question—if all of this is so simple, why do so many people still complain that they lack self-confidence and that they seem to be powerless to change that?

It happens for a number of reasons, but the most important is not accepting one's uncertainty and expecting to somehow induce self-confidence solely by the effort of a strong will. But life simply isn't that way, and in order to feel confident, you need to gather a whole bunch of experiences related to a certain area, which means that it's necessary to **leave the safe harbor and sail to deep waters**, thus facing uncertainty.

If you demand self-confidence from yourself, then you focus on what you are feeling at that moment, which results in a tendency to make yourself feel guilty (because you're not self-confident already), which in turn makes the whole thing much more difficult. Then the risk related to taking action on an unknown ground rises, because now, not only do you not know what the effect of your activity will be, but you are also paying too much attention to how you will feel, and not knowing if you will start feeling confident soon enough upsets you.

Then, apart from the uncertainty, you could also start feeling angry at yourself; you might start criticizing yourself, and thus start thinking that other people are or will soon be criticizing you as well. Now, your attention is not focused solely on the task at hand or your mission, but also on all your unnecessary or even detrimental thoughts and feelings. Your brainpower is being wasted on making a big problem out of a little problem. It is really difficult and discouraging to keep encountering the same situation again and again.

So the first step to self-confidence is, paradoxically, accepting your uncertainty!

You must see it as reasonable, strictly necessary and... transient.

When you're entering unknown ground, trespassing in an area which is not yours, into unknown activities, it's OBVIOUS and unavoidable that you will feel uncertain and doubtful. **Instead of demanding from yourself that you start feeling confident right now, just continue taking action and pursuing your goal.**

People so often give so much weight to the feelings accompanying new activities that they postpone action until they magically start feeling confident one day, which equals postponing action forever, **because self-confidence is a result of taking action, not a prerequisite for it!**

"Thinking will not overcome fear, but action will."

– W Clement Stone

What self-confidence is and what it is not

The correct understanding of the word "self-confidence" and all the terms connected with it is a foundation you need to cover if you want to effectively start working on it. Most people have a very hazy picture of what self-confidence, self-esteem, self-acceptance, etc. really are.

These terms are confused with each other and used interchangeably in many books and on many blogs, which keeps people from seeing a clear picture of how to start working on their self-confidence and self-esteem.

Take this chapter as a map showing a general image of the process of gaining self-confidence. I will tell you in which elements of self-development and self-work you should engage to start building a deep, natural and ever-lasting sense of self-esteem and confidence.

What self-confidence is NOT

Self-confidence IS NOT about arrogance, exaltation, believing "I am better than others," acting like a "king of the hill," or treating others without kindness and empathy. Such childish behaviors and attitudes are often confused with self-confidence, and people who make this kind of false judgment form an obstacle in their heads. Some of these people simply do not want to become another arrogant douchebag tool or stuck-up bitch (and that's a good thing), but as long as arrogance equals confidence in their understanding, they are the ones blocking themselves from achieving deep, healthy and natural confidence.

Moreover, self-confidence is not an **absolute absence of fear and self-doubt**. Self-confident people simply know that they have to act apart from that fear, and know how to do that. Hence, self-confidence is not some "promised land" of totally unrestricted courage or bravery, thanks to which you are able to convince anyone of anything, realize every one of your goals or save the entire world. Imagining self-confidence like that **paradoxically makes it harder for you to achieve it**, as we all subconsciously know that such a state of mind is simply not achievable for human beings as a constant thing (unless you are very drunk way too often).

SO what IS self-confidence?

There is no one clear definition of self-confidence; that's why I will tell you about its most important foundations, which, in my opinion, describe self-confidence in a complete and comprehensive way:

Self-confidence is:
1. **The ability to act despite the fear and doubts that are inside you**; the ability to get out of your

comfort zone; the ability to cope with the challenges of everyday life.
2. Knowledge about how to do something and the certainty that you can actually use that skill in a practical situation.
3. The ability to stand up for your own rights; the ability to defend yourself verbally and maybe physically.

The self-esteem part of the term "self-confidence" is:

4. **Feeling good in your own skin**, not only physically—e.g., in your body—but generally—feeling good about yourself, as a person. To put it differently—having a positive evaluation of yourself, liking yourself, having a healthy relationship with yourself, treating yourself as your own best friend.
5. **Treating yourself as a valuable person** (which is the foundation of the feeling of self-worth); having an unbiased perception of your strengths and talents; having an appreciation of these, taking pride and joy in them, being grateful for them and able to talk about them without false modesty.
6. **Practicing self-forgiveness and self-understanding;** having the ability to forgive yourself for your mistakes and accept your flaws and imperfections (and being aware that **everyone** has flaws and imperfections).

Of course we could add a few more factors to this definition, such as acting freely and authentically among people, but I know from my experience that they come naturally when the above conditions are met. As you can see, the concepts of self-esteem, self-worth and self-acceptance are directly related to the concept of self-confidence. Later in this book I will further expand on that connection and explain it much more deeply.

Self-confidence as an emotion

Self-confidence, as an emotion, is very fleeting. You can learn how to be naturally self-confident "just because," and become very relaxed and calm in almost every situation.

The key is to accept all the black scenarios your mind is used to coming up with. Let me explain to you a mechanism you didn't even know existed. This awareness will give you the potential to free yourself from any kind of uncertainty.

Confidence is usually defined as a concrete emotion, thanks to which you feel you can do anything and nothing will stop you. However, it's worth remembering that this kind of emotion is very unstable and fleeting; one moment you could be pumped up and psyched with courage, just to find that all of it evaporates a few minutes later. That's why we have to look at self-confidence differently and view it as something a little bit more complex than just an emotion. That's how you can access the same feeling on a much deeper and more permanent level.

First, let me explain a few very important mechanisms that operate in people's minds. The very first thing you ought to know is that it isn't all about inducing the exact emotion of confidence. Of course, that can be done in many different ways, but the state won't last long. **Lack of confidence** is, in all reality, a state in which you **are afraid of something or you feel endangered**. When you erase this fear or feeling of danger, you will **automatically start feeling calm and relaxed**. And that's the confidence that appears spontaneously—when you get rid of negative emotions.

This kind of self-confidence is much more solid and persistent than a mere induced emotion. Emotions can also be useful—they allow you to conquer your fear in a moment you might really need to, but the fear will still stay somewhere in your head, hiding and waiting for a good moment to start haunting you again. Thus the key to real peace and confidence is **to get rid of fear and doubt and acquire the feeling of familiarity**. Then you don't have to induce any emotional state at all. The strong feeling of **self-confidence is then a natural part of yourself.** It's like in theater—when the curtain rises, it shows something that has been there for a long time already.

The overprotective mind and useless fear

So where does the lack of self-confidence come from? The human mind is a creation that loves safety. **It does everything possible just to avoid any feeling of danger and to keep the status quo.** Unfortunately, in most cases it does much more than needed. To shield us from any unfavorable turn of events, it launches various unnecessary security measures in many life situations.

I'm talking about mechanisms like fear, crushing stress, difficulties trusting other people, negative images in your head, paralyzing and negative self-talk. That's why some people don't know what to say when they are trying to make new friends. Others feel paralyzing stress in their bodies and feel their throats clenching just when they are about to give a public speech to a huge audience. Or when they are studying for exams, they start imagining what will happen if they fail. And anytime they are about to undertake a challenge, their internal voice tells them all the excuses one could possibly imagine.

Take a moment to think how your lack of self-confidence shows. **Is it that you "don't have" the self-confidence to even start something?** Or is it perhaps just that in a given situation, you start thinking about black scenarios, you start timid-voiced self-talks, you come up with hundreds of excuses, you lie to yourself and focus all your mind power on what could possibly go wrong?

Properly developed emotional intelligence is a very important matter here. It's like good oil to your internal engine. You can have a brand new Lamborghini, but without oil, the expensive engine will get wrecked in no time. One good way to remove these internal obstacles, which are analogous to a handbrake that's still engaged while you're driving the Lamborghini, is to change your internal dialogues and make friends with your internal critic. I describe this and many other interesting methods in my other book, "Emotional Intelligence Training," which is a must-read supplement to this book.

Now, it's very important to understand that your mind's intention is positive. In bringing up all the things that take your confidence away, it simply wants to protect you from any danger. What your subconscious mind doesn't fully follow, though, is that we live in the twenty-first century, not in the Paleolithic era, so in most cases it misjudges the situation you find yourself in and simply overprotects you—unnecessarily.

Because, really, can meeting new people be dangerous? Maybe if you go to the worst area of your town drunk and start behaving aggressively, kicking people and peeing on cars, or start abusing women married to local gangsters, but otherwise? It's absolutely safe—if you act normal and civilized, according to widely understood social norms. Will giving an imperfect public speech make people start throwing rotten eggs and sharp knives at you, aiming at your throat and forehead? Even if you fail an exam, will the world collapse or will you lose your health? Everything would be fine if not for these unnecessary "safety measures" and "security systems" your subconscious mind decides to use altogether too often, stopping you from acting normally and proactively changing your life.

So, how do you get rid of them and restore or gain strong self-confidence? However hard it might sound, accept all the obstacles your mind creates. Later in this book I will show you effective exercises that will help you do that. For now, you need to make a decision to accept them. The moment you feel real and deep acceptance of all the black scenarios you tend to think about and of all the bad feelings you feel in your body, the resistance will disappear immediately. Does it mean the bad feelings won't be there anymore? No, you might still feel stressed out, but you will stop feeling paralyzed or held back and will start taking action.

Acceptance is a synonym of safety, in the understanding of your subconscious mind. When you totally accept that, for example, your audience might laugh at you when you get awkward during your speech, then the threat is gone, according to your mind. Lack of acceptance is the source of supposed danger. When you come to acceptance, it makes the supposed danger disappear. This process is not even entirely about self-acceptance—self-acceptance often comes automatically, when you accept the negative scenarios constantly appearing in your head.

How do you do that in real life? **It's simply about reconciling and making peace with any negative vision of possible consequence your mind might have created.** You need to say to yourself, "OK, if that happens, I will understand and accept it," and you need to say it a lot. You have to really feel the reconciliation; you have to feel that you **don't need** the resistance anymore. You have to feel that **even if** this scenario really happens, it won't really affect you. You will still be healthy and alive.

The procedure is simple. When your mind comes up with a negative consequence of any of your actions, you don't resist, you don't tilt at windmills, but accept it. This applies to every situation in your life. Most problems in people's lives don't come from the fact that they feel stressed out because of something or are afraid of doing something. **The real pain comes from the fact that they tend to make a problem out of that stress and fear.** So they literally make a problem out of a problem, on a daily basis, almost every single time. "Oh, it's so stressful, I shouldn't be so stressed out!" Maybe you should, maybe you shouldn't, but you are. So stop obsessing over it, focusing on it and overblowing it.

People write black scenarios in their heads when they are about to meet new people, when they give public speeches, when they want to start a new business or register their company, when they want to leave home and start traveling, when they are getting ready for a date, when they study for their exams, when... We could go on like that forever. These negative visions, when not accepted, are a constant source of bad emotions. These emotions destroy your peace and your perceived self-confidence along with the positive energy you could use to take action. Accept every single of these bad scenarios, and you will be really surprised how swiftly you see a big change in your life.

Some time ago I met a man very concerned and scared about what people might think about him during conversations. It made communication and relations with other people extremely difficult because the feeling of insecurity was always holding him back from acting naturally, instead of like an awkward alien from Alpha Centauri. All his fear was initiated and constantly kept alive by this one, specific thought he had during conversations: "This person will probably think something bad about me." In a moment we defined what the real consequences of people thinking bad things about him might be, and then we worked a little bit toward accepting these silly consequences, and all his fear disappeared in a matter of minutes.

Useless fear

Self-confidence means thinking the right way and doing the right things (both in your head and in real life), things that counteract the fear of unknown. Nowadays fear is the main factor sabotaging the vast majority, if not all, of our actions. Thousands of years ago, when our ancestors were fighting for survival in the forests and deserts, fear was very important and it helped our species survive. Unfortunately, in modern times, this state of mind dominates most people's lives and doesn't let them function normally.

In 99% of cases the fear you feel is useless and irrational. Times have changed, but we are still afraid of the most harmless and usual situations. How many times have you been afraid of an exam or a meeting with a stranger? What was the outcome of this fear? Isn't it true that you would be much better off if you were able to keep calm and push the fear away? Confidence is not only useful in everyday life and casual situations. Do you want to fulfill your dreams? Big achievements require brave and fearless actions. If you want to act brave, you need to be confident.

Let's now look at self-confidence as a proper approach to the world around you. Only changing your approach and your mindset will give you access to a permanent feeling of confidence at a really deep level. That's definitely something to focus on.

Later in this book, I will also show you a few effective exercises to increase your self-confidence at an emotional level. You have to remember that self-confidence can be either **a permanent state of mind**, a part of your identity, **or an emotion, which can come and go**. It's good to know how to trigger such emotions, and in the last part of the book, I will also show you ways to "imprint" these emotions in your subconscious and to "anchor" them, so you can access them at any time, but the **most important thing is to change your mindset,** so there's no more space for the fear of the unknown and the fear of taking action.

The primal fear

Does the fear of failing makes you feel petrified and keep you from achieving your goals? So many people live way below their capabilities just because they fear they could fail while going for what they want! Let me show you how to get rid of this feeling and start taking on big challenges. You will change your way of thinking about failure, and moreover—you will grow to like it!

The feeling of fear, by definition, has a positive intention to it—its function is to save you from the negative effects that come from some of your actions. Fear, in general, is NOT useless in our lives. It is needed when we are in situations that threaten our life or health. It's a great source of motivation and a performance booster, as you will read about later in this book. It also stops us from performing actions that might end badly for us—think of the fear of heights or spiders, for instance. Why are we so afraid of little, fragile spiders? They don't have the strength and power of a wild cat; they have neither the brute mass of a gorilla, nor a heavy armor. You can crush a spider with one stomp, if you have your shoes on. The vast majority of spiders can't kill you or even harm you in any major way, if you live in a temperate climate, and the same goes for snakes. But somehow almost all people on Earth, even in the polar territories where there are hardly any insects or arachnids at all, are subconsciously afraid of them.

It was hardwired in our ancestors' brains thousands and thousands of years ago, when all humans lived in small groups in the African bush. Since there were no hospitals, no antibiotics, no advanced medicines (maybe a shaman could help, and maybe not), no vaccines, no real painkillers, no thick jeans and no shoes, all the small bugs and spiders could kill them in a matter of seconds, especially in the dark. One spider, scorpion or snake bite meant paralysis, agony and extreme suffering for hours. And in the meantime, other insects and animals would surely join in eating the poor caveman alive, in the gloomy darkness. Can you imagine? With all the modern advancements, this fear is hugely outdated these days (unless you live in a tropical climate and are extremely unlucky, etc.), but no wonder the "code" in our genes it still active.

Exactly the same goes for the fear of public speaking, talking to strangers, meeting people of the opposite sex, saying something stupid, making a fool out of yourself, etc.—it all comes from thousands of years ago. In these times, you could get exiled or killed for a behavior that offended a shaman, a prime warrior, the fiery forest goddess of Zulu-Bulu-Gulu, or, in the worst case, the local chief, or if what you said was simply perceived as dangerous, inappropriate or blasphemous. None of these dangers are real or actual in today's Western society, but again, "the code" is still active in our genes and it's messing with people's heads. The simple realization of the fact that we've been running on outdated software for a long time now can be a big liberation.

The society-induced fear

Moreover, not only are we still haunted and held back by the most primitive fears, but somehow the fear as such has managed to sneak in and access practical every single area of our lives. How did that happen?

Remember your elementary school days? Since your youngest years, you were taught that mistakes are very bad. By inflicting negative emotions when a student does something wrong, teachers successfully install the idea that failures should be feared and avoided at all costs. That's how the fear settled down where it is totally useless, and sometimes even really detrimental. Today, as an adult, you might know that mistakes can be good, on a logical level, but as a little kid, you subconsciously and unconditionally believed your teachers, your parents, the "TV people," local authorities, etc. You were mentally defenseless. At the same time, similar programming often takes place in temples (churches, mosques, synagogues, etc.). While adult people understand the power of analogies, metaphors, symbols, and parables and comprehend the hidden and often complicated meaning of art, children DO NOT get that. Even if you somehow explained what's going on to a three- or five-year-old kid who barely speaks his own language, their subconscious mind (and it's developing at an amazing pace during the first years of life) doesn't know what's going on. So every time a child hears, "You were born sinful," "Our sins make our god angry/sad/disappointed in you/us," "If you offend our god, you will go to hell and suffer forever," "If you are not a good Christian/Muslim/Jew and think too much about pretty girls, you will make God very sad/angry," "Money is a bad devilish thing and rich people shall be miserable," etc., he or she **subconsciously takes it for granted**. One or two times shouldn't be too harmful, but if this is repeated every week for years, the repercussions in adult life can be terrifying. Sometimes a very short remark from someone a kid treats as an authority can **totally**

wreck their self-esteem for long, long years. If you don't believe me, look up the "Monster Study" experiment that was performed on 22 orphan children in Davenport, Iowa in 1939. You will find lots of exhaustive info about it with a simple Google search. You might be surprised and horrified at the same time. Once you do that, imagine what happens when guilt, shame and fear (even of the most natural and normal things) are inflicted again, again and again on a fragile and defenseless mind, for many long years.

Do you remember what I wrote about how crappy radio music puts you in a state of low consciousness and even semi-hypnosis? The same goes for religious rituals, chanting, repeating long mantras in a crowd, etc. Why are the rituals in some religions or sects so long and so prone to making people feel sleepy or tired? Is the almighty, loving and infinitely ultra-intelligent Entity, who has created the entire Universe, really happier or more satisfied, just because people have been forcing themselves to stand or kneel in a temple for two hours instead of twenty minutes? Really think about it.

The reason I'm mentioning it is because that, among other things, was what happened to me when I was a little kid. I had been an acolyte in a local church for many years and my mom was (and still is) a very, or maybe even extremely, religious person. The experience of serving the church was nice; I met many friends, but I remember that at some point I started feeling a big, deep and gloomy fear inside of myself. I couldn't let it go, no matter how hard I tried. I was feeling guilty and terrified, like something very dark was about to come into my life. The state persisted in me for three years. At one point I was so extremely scared I couldn't sleep or eat; I would mainly just drink water. I remember the nights when I lied in my bed, wet like a boat disaster survivor because I was sweating so much, feeling my heart beating so hard I felt it could jump out of my chest or kill me with a stroke at any time. Once I looked in the mirror and I was pale like a kelpie. I could hardly catch my breath. I was about nine years old at the time it started. I never experienced such a strong and deep fear later in my life.

Doctors said I was physically healthy (although at one point I had lots of symptoms of diabetes) and the problem was in my head. The main reason I felt that brutal, devastating fear for so many years was that I was feeling shame and guilt just because I started growing up and being naturally attracted to girls. I felt the fiery need to kiss them, like actors in the romantic movies I saw, touch them or watch pictures of nude women. At the same time, I was sure that would offend God and make him very sad or angry. The normal and natural thing every boy and girl starts feeling at a certain age was turned into an obnoxious, perverted and cruel crime in my consciousness with the invaluable help of church, teachers and my own mum. **It wasn't my fault and I did nothing wrong, but I didn't know that at the time.**

Additionally, I once heard from a priest, and also read in some kind of "how to get to heaven tutorial 101," that masturbation was one of the worst sins a kid could commit in the eyes of God. Obviously, I was extremely ashamed of confessing these things to an older man; there was no Internet back then and no one to talk to about it, so sometimes I would force myself to confess it (and then feel humiliated and ashamed), but other times I would omit it, and felt that I had offended God, lied to a servant of God and shown my filth and cowardice, and that I would go to hell to burn in the eternal fire. At that point, I developed an obsession with fire. I was literally terrified of catching ablaze and dying in flames, even though I wasn't a fireman, there was no war and it wasn't a real threat.

Every single time I even forgot to tell a single terrifying "sin" (like "Father, I said the 'f-word' once this month"), I would feel the same crushing emotion. The religious lessons in school didn't help either. I can't count how many times the "teacher" scared us with visions of hell or told us about the saints who supposedly, with God's protection, went down to see the atrocities of hell with their own eyes and then went back to tell people how filthy and bad their nature (which they didn't create in the first place) is and how their filthy essence and deeds hurt God.

It took me about four or five years to overcome the heavy shackles of the paralyzing fear and the bitter guilt, but many consequences were still present many years after that happened, for example during my middle and high school years. When I was 13, I met a very smart monk who lived in a monastery placed high in the mountains, and also one very fair and down-to-earth priest. They explained the whole thing to me and told me that human sexuality and sexual attraction are natural, beautiful, God-sent and not shameful or frightening, but it was already way too late. The harm was done and part of "my little soul" was taken. There are no words to describe how extremely scared and guilty I had felt for so many years.

Now, I'm not saying priests of any religion are doing this on purpose to harm kids (maybe they do; maybe they don't; you and I don't know for sure) or that you should never go to your temple again. I'm not trying to convert anyone to anything in particular, but you just need to know that this is often exactly where a big part of the unexplainable fear, guilt, anger or sorrow we have in us comes from.

Parents also play a BIG and crucial role in this process, so it's not all on the religions of the world, but still, every single element counts a lot. You need to be aware of what might cause the fears and limitations that block you and make your life worse or sometimes downright miserable.

Anyway, if you still don't believe me, then don't believe me. Buy a couple of good psychology books about the topics of consciousness, subconscious, and the development of children's brains during the first years of life; read academic research papers from all around the world including the best colleges and universities; educate yourself about the power of hypnosis and subliminal messages, and you will find the truth on your own.

Today, your subconscious is still that little kid. Maybe a scared one. You might know something and it might even be **obvious** to you, **but the kid inside of your brain doesn't know it.** By the way, that's where the name of the entire category "inner child" comes from. The "inner child" is the kid inside of you. Your subconscious literally is a little boy or a little girl.

This imprinted fear of failing and the feelings of shame and inherent guilt make people act irrationally—they avoid taking actions that could change their lives for the better, because they are afraid that their actions won't change anything or will make the situation even worse. They are also afraid that their friends will laugh at them, their family will be let down, they will feel guilty, ashamed, or they will keep hearing, "You shouldn't have done that!" in their head until they die. Or that they can't change anything, because "that's what god wants" and "that's just my fate." No, it isn't.

And that's exactly why people are stuck in difficult situations for years and years, living their boring and unsatisfying lives, sweating at the mere thought of taking any action or making any change at all. People hold back from starting businesses, investing money, making public appearances, making new friends, and achieving their dream goals. **Just because they are afraid!**

Do you want to be one of these people, paralyzed by fear at the mere thought of taking any action toward changing bad things in your life?

The prize for letting the fear go

Only when you decide to let go of that fear and start acting in spite of it will you start actually doing something to change your life for the better. That's the most important step leading to any life success. **You will start acting, motivated by faith in your success, full of enthusiasm and energy.**

What you have to do is to anchor positive feelings to taking new challenges, so anytime a new idea appears in your head, along comes the thought, "Yes! I want to do it! I will make that happen! I will be successful!" This thought will push you towards immediate action. And even if you fail the first time, nothing bad will happen. You will say to yourself, "OK, I did this wrong, but I did that correctly; I need to fix these, and quit those"… and then you will stand up, brush off and start acting accordingly. **Thanks to this approach you will ultimately be successful, no matter what your goal is.** You will be happier, knowing that you didn't let the fear of failure stop you from doing what you really want to do in life.

How to get rid of the fear of failure

Taking a good approach to things is crucial here. Apart from that, there are a few things you can do to almost totally erase your fear of failure. But let's start with the good beliefs first.

Remember, <u>mindset is the king:</u>

1. There are no failures; there's just feedback. Write this belief on a piece of paper, hang it in someplace visible and make it the way you look at all your failures. It's time to understand that failures are extraordinarily precious. Each failure brings lots of wisdom and a valuable lesson to learn.

"If you want to increase your success rate, double your failure rate "

– Thomas J. Watson

If something doesn't work out, it's a sign that it should be done differently. So, with that knowledge, you are a huge step closer to success. Thomas Edison created hundreds of unsuccessful bulb projects before he managed to come up with a working bulb. Now he's "immortal"—he will forever be remembered as the man who had invented the lightbulb. If he had been afraid of failure, he wouldn't have taken his chances. And even if he had, he would probably have been discouraged after a few failed tries.

The key is to look at failures as a result of your actions. If the result is different from what you planned, it's a great occasion for you to learn—next time you will do something differently. **You've gained a new experience, and experience is what builds self-confidence.** Remember that almost every single road to success leads through failures—that's the natural way things are**, an obvious part of the process**. If you want to succeed in anything at all, you have to learn many new things, and there's no better teacher than a failure! This mindset is an absolutely necessary basis when it comes to achieving any goals in life. The point is to take **calculated risks,** so when you fail, you can go past it. Always ask yourself, "What's the worst thing that can happen?" Write it down on a piece of paper and ask yourself if you can handle it, and if you can, how exactly will you go past that problem. And then… TAKE ACTION!

2. Imagine the consequences ten years from now of constantly quitting any life challenges today. How do you think your life will look if you stay stuck in this fear of failure, and you never take your chances or any risks at all?

Now, imagine that you always take advantage of every single possibility that comes to you and the ones that you create. Imagine yourself accepting many different, new challenges. Imagine that the calculated risks you've taken have paid off—you've become successful in what you wanted. Take a moment to imagine your life 15 years from now, if you manage to get rid of the useless fear of failure. Visualize it.

Now: **Which life do you chose?**

Moreover, you have to use the powers of both positive and negative motivation and the power of visualization to drive you and give you strength.

Take action now and write down all the situations when, because of your low confidence, you lost a great opportunity to do something remarkable, or something you really wanted to do, meet someone, go somewhere you wanted to go or change something important in your life. This will be your negative motivation.

Now, focus on the positive motivation!

Write down all the experiences that will be easily attainable for you once your confidence is much higher. For example, you might want to make a public speech on a topic important to you, start your own business, take a hitchhiking trip all around Europe or America, date a stunningly beautiful woman or a handsome devil, and so on. Imagine them very clearly, as vividly as you can. Do it regularly. You have to realize that they really are within your reach. They could be realized in a relatively short time—you don't need to wait a couple of years to make them real! Really think about how great it would be to bring some of them into your life in three or four months! Imagine yourself a couple of months or even weeks from now, when you're already doing each of these things, and immerse yourself in all the good emotions coming from the experience!

Also, do this exercise:

Think of a moment in your life when you felt true power. When you knew nothing could stand in your way, that you could handle anything. When you felt courage and strength, and maybe also pride in being who you are. It could even be a scene from a long time ago. Close your eyes and remember this situation very carefully. Recall the situation; imagine it as vividly as possible and, step by step, start remembering all the details—see what you saw then, hear what you heard, remember the smells, colors, and so on. Notice as your power starts to appear—an unstoppable force, a volcano of energy. Locate it—where in your body does it appear? Where is it going? If you were to give it a shape and color, what would they be?

Once you have the power inside of you and you can feel it, think about situations from your future, situations of future successes you want to appreciate right now. Think about a success you plan to have next month, something on your way to greater confidence, or some goal of yours that is connected to that. Choose anything that drives you. For example, you could imagine yourself making friends with a magnificent person. Feeling the power inside of your body now, see how much more fully you are able to appreciate your great success. Feel the pride that comes from the fact of accomplishing your goal and getting closer to your dreams and use this pride to reinforce your sense of power. **Learn how to truly appreciate your successes, and you will set your whole body and mind to start and keep achieving them!**

3. If you have always been afraid to lose until now, I strongly suspect that anytime you were just about to start anything at all, you kept imagining what could possibly go wrong. For example, you imagined how you would fail your oral exams in college; how the professor would say, "I'm sorry, but your knowledge is insufficient. You just flunked"; how you go away full of resentment and disappointment. These pointless daydreams are the main source of fuel for your fear.

That's why from now on you're always going to imagine the best case scenario possible! ALWAYS visualize every single situation you are about to go through ending with successes. Sit down for a couple of minutes, **relax,** close your eyes and start imagining what you are about to go through. In this particular example, you might see how the examiner smiles to you and says, "Congratulations, you have passed!" Feel your wide smile as well, and feel your great joy. Imagine your friends congratulating you as you receive your diploma. This simple visualization exercise will give you lots of motivation and self-belief, making fear of failure diminish greatly.

4. Don't make it personal. If something goes wrong, it doesn't mean that something is wrong with you! It could be a sign that your actions might be not perfectly calibrated or planned. Or it might be just bad luck—welcome to real life! You just need to change your actions to achieve success. Definitely too many people create bad opinions about themselves when they fail. You need to avoid this mistake, because failure rarely says anything at all about your character or capabilities, but almost always says something about the actions and strategy you took and the preparations you made.

What to do to develop your self-confidence every day

I've noticed that indecisive people, sooner or later, usually come to the realization that something's wrong with them in terms of not having enough self-confidence, and they finally start taking action. Very often, though, instead of taking small steps, they take big hops and start doing things that might be considered "hardcore" by the majority of our society. When I first came to the realization I needed to start working on my self-confidence and self-esteem, I at one point delved into doing extreme things. For example, when I was traveling in Bolivia, I went down from the top floor of a 25-floor building[1], with both

---

[1] You can look it up: "Urban Rush, La Paz, Bolivia"

feet on the building's slippery wall (it was raining), head down, attached to the roof only by a single line, which was linked to my harness with a metal hook. When I was somewhere in the middle, people on the rooftop disabled the lock and I started falling at full speed, head down. It was a planned part of the rap jumping "fun" and probably absolutely safe, but obviously my brain was convinced I would die in a moment. I was so scared I almost fainted and puked at the same time, but I did it twice… and the second time was even worse. Another time, when I was traveling in former Soviet territory, I decided I wanted to try some paragliding. I found a guy from the Ukraine who was a semi-pro in this beautiful sport and we spent 40 minutes flying over 300 meters above the ground, doing extreme twists and tricks. I was so scared I shouted out loud. Also, when I was visiting my parents in my hometown, I decided to talk my friends into climbing an old and creepy 230-foot GSM broadcast transmitter tower, which once was a power plant chimney. During my childhood and teenage years, I would observe its silhouette protruding from the forest and its gloomily shining red lights through my room's window at nights, wondering how it would be to climb it one day, before I left town and went to college. We eventually did it one day at twilight, many years after I had graduated from college and left my country. We climbed it without any security measures at all—no lines, no gloves and no harness, unprepared. There were no middle levels or stops, just a continuous long ladder, leading straight up to the top. It was all worth it in terms of gaining new unforgettable experiences and acting against my fear, especially since I used to have a very strong fear of heights, but at the same time, it was really stupid and I or any of my friends could well be dead now if something had gone wrong. The errors of youth you don't regret, after all. Why am I telling you this? Well, it was a nice adventure to do all these crazy and sometimes dumb things and I would still like to try some parachute jumping, **but truth be told**—after having faced all these fears—**my everyday confidence remained practically unchanged!** I did these things because I thought they would make it easier for me to talk to people, give public speeches, and have difficult conversations, but these fears haven't magically disappeared. Quite obviously, you will feel a big boost in your self-confidence for a moment (or maybe even entire day, if you do something really scary)—I remember having one of the best nights out ever back there in La Paz, Bolivia, after we went down twice from that block tower with our heads down. But the following day, the adrenaline rush wore off and we felt perfectly normal.

That being said, there are much better, easier and safer methods of developing your self-confidence, and you can do it systematically, every day—as opposed to in extreme sports and events. What's that? Every single time you are afraid of something—DO IT. You can practice bungee jumping every other week, but still be extremely scared when you need to talk to a stranger or talk to your boss about giving you a raise or quitting your job. Believe me, this fear won't disappear once you jump out of a plane enough times. It will still be there. So, if you need to do something—DO IT, against your fear. Everybody's afraid. If someone's never afraid, they need psychiatric intervention. Self-confident people are just those who have learned to act against their fear or even make friends with their fear—this is the true art, as opposed to hiding beneath your fear your entire life.

Facing the fear

People usually tend to run away from their fears, instead of facing them. Paradoxically, once you face your fears, you will usually feel excitement and other good emotions—happiness, liberation, joy and adventure—which will continue to appear more frequently in your life afterwards.

It's funny how we often are the ones making ourselves scared, like cats and dogs attacking their own tails. When I first decided to quit the corporate job in which I felt I wouldn't last much longer because I was underpaid and overall not happy with it, it took me three months of everyday struggle to finally make my decision. I would go through many different lists of pros and cons, through imaginary scenarios of myself handing a resignation letter to my boss and telling my colleagues I quit (which made me feel amazingly great every single time), but I still was afraid to just trust myself. Long story short, I could've done it much faster and saved myself months of battling with my own mind. Once I really quit, there's no way to describe how light, easy, happy and free I felt. People think that they are afraid of quitting their job, starting their own business, meeting new people, forming a relationship, etc., but these fears are usually superficial.

The main driving force behind your problems usually lies much deeper below the surface level. If you want to make yourself more aware of the things that are really stopping you, take a sheet of paper and a pen and try to write down everything you are afraid of in your life. No matter what situations make you afraid, try to write down EVERY SINGLE ONE. Once you have your list ready, take a few moments to deeply reflect on what it really is that you are afraid of. For example, you might have written down that you are afraid of giving public speeches—but you can't really be afraid of giving a public speech as such, can you? It's not a war; nobody will start shooting you; you are perfectly safe, and you know that. What you can be afraid of, though, is, for instance, being criticized, failing (not being able to finish your speech), other people judging you, laughing at you, etc. Most importantly, you could spend countless hours working on your diction, and know your presentation perfectly well, but the stage fright will appear anyway, because the real, main fear—for example, the fear of rejection or being laughed at—wasn't worked through.

The fear that appeared to be the "main" fear—stage fright and fear of public appearances—might be, and usually is, just a surface problem, underneath which other fears are hiding—fear that harsh criticism will be too crushing to cope with, or that you will never be given the chance to give a public speech again, etc. The same goes for the fear of meeting new people. For example, men are very often afraid of approaching and naturally meeting women, because they think extraordinarily evil things might happen to them. However, usually it all boils down to the fear of rejection, not the fear of approaching a woman and simply having a basic conversation with her. So often people chose not to approach and meet new people, running away from the fear of rejection, at the same time not noticing that by not approaching they induce bad emotions in themselves and, in a sense, reject themselves, making it GUARANTEED that they will never meet the other person. In short, they make their emotions even worse by their own thought processes.

Once you have all your fears written down, take a few moments to think what might be hidden underneath them, what your core fear is in all this. Once you're done doing that, you can ask yourself a few very useful questions. I write "useful," because when you face your fears, you will feel much better knowing the answers to these questions. At the same time, I don't want to lie to you by saying that your fears will disappear all of a sudden and completely—there are no "magic pills"—but you will have it much easier!

Important question #1: "What's the worst possible thing that can happen if I mess up?" For example, "During my speech everyone will start laughing at me when I stutter"—ask yourself if this has ever happened to you in the past, and if this is possible at all. If you are going to give your speech to an audience interested in the topic, they will just continue to listen. Even if you stutter once in a while or say something wrong, the most likely scenario is that no one will laugh and absolutely nothing will happen. Probably no one will even notice and people will just wait in silence until you get back on track... unless you are planning on doing something unusual and ridiculous, like giving a speech about "how our government loves us" in a penitentiary full of drunk convicts, or talk about the gifts of the Kamasutra to a group of five-year-old kids. It's very good to ask yourself these questions, as the vast majority of our fears are illusory and once they are disassembled into parts and explored enough, most of them just disappear and we can approach each issue with peace of mind.

Important question #2: "I'm curious, what will happen if I do that?" Just by asking yourself this question, you redirect your fear into curiosity. Maybe it won't be curiosity like a four-year-old kid feels when discovering our world, but still this emotion is very useful and interesting when combined with fear, creating a new emotion, some combination of intrigue and excitement, which is rather stimulating and helps us take action and move forward.

Once you have asked yourself these questions and thought about the answers, the best advice I can give you is to finally START DOING THE THINGS THAT SCARE YOU. That's the only way to confront your illusory and exaggerated fears with reality, which dissolves them, like hot water dissolves a snowball put into a sink. You can't count on your fear disappearing in a matter of seconds or maybe even hours, but every single time you do the thing that scares you, the fear will be diminished. For instance, you will be given feedback from the people you performed in front of; you will see that many of them liked your speeches or concerts, that despite a few stumbles you were able to finish your speech without any big problems, that you are still alive, that you still have your arms and legs, that people still like you, etc.

The same applies to meeting men and women, making new friends, dating, traveling on your own, partying, starting businesses, etc. You have to notice and disassemble your fear, and then act apart from the fact you can still feel the fear. If it doesn't go away after, for instance, a few minutes of conversation and if you feel really overwhelmed, you can simply say so to the people you are talking with, as I stated earlier in this book. After all, you want these people to get to know your real self, not your fake mask and superficial personality, and you want to be real with yourself. It's an effective, simple and honest method. Honesty with yourself is the king. It won't necessary lead you into making a great impression on these people at first, and you might feel like an even bigger weirdo; they may see that you are really anxious, so don't expect miracles to happen. However, in this way you are unblocking yourself, gradually progressing and feeling more at ease, throwing your fake masks away and learning to act despite feeling bad.

Instead of acting like you are not afraid in all social situations, you show your cards, accepting the fact that you are afraid. You don't have to make a main attraction out of the fact that you're scared and overblow it, but just admit it. Yep, I feel nervous but it's nothing too bad. That's usually the moment when your fear starts going away. As it turns out, so often our biggest fear when meeting other people or getting out of our comfort zone is what other people might think or do when you screw up (for example, when people walking down the street see that an attractive girl you approached ignored you and now they know you're not a Casanova but just a regular Joe).

Also, in reality, you are often afraid of these strangers' actual behaviors, not of what they think. People might think something bad but not actually do anything, and that's usually what happens. So, for instance, a guy could be scared either by the thought that a girl he wants to meet will think he's an idiot (which is a rare fear), or much more likely by the thought that she might slap him in the face or start shouting, "LOOK, OVER HERE—A BORING IMBECILE!!!" ...which, in my experience, never happens. When I noticed this fear in myself, I decided to approach people despite the fear in my core and what was happening around me (e.g., a lot of traffic and people passing me by). Gradually, I started feeling more and more confident in these situations, and again, despite the fear that still was there I would ask people what they were thinking when a stranger approached them, how they felt, how their day was, how they would feel if they had to start a conversation with a total stranger, etc. What

I received in exchange was REALITY, as opposed to the fake and illusory fears created in my head as a result of separation from reality. After some time, I didn't have to do these things anymore, but by then my fear was almost completely crushed. I learned that most people you come across in your life don't give a shit about what you do, who you are or what your life is like. And those who do are often absolutely irrelevant.

By the way, when, some time ago, one of your friends supposedly said or did something stupid, did you remember it one hour later? One day later? One week later? Would you remember a stranger saying a silly thing or failing at something? One day later? One week later? Wouldn't you have your own problems and your own life to worry about? Yeah, that's right. People don't even remember. They don't care. They couldn't care less.

It can't be said enough—the key to healthy self-confidence is activity. The more action you take, the more experienced you become and the more feedback you can gather, both about your resources and your restrictions.

Real knowledge (not conjectures) about "what I can do" and "what I can't do" is a foundation of healthy self-esteem, and what goes along with it, healthy self-confidence.

Start taking action—simple advice, but if you've been looking for an answer to the question "How can I be self-confident?," you surely know that activity and action are the last things you feel like doing, mainly because of your fear of failure.

You are constantly postponing activity, always deciding that you will start taking action once you start feeling better. The problem here is that you can't start feeling better without taking action, so you remain stuck in a deadlock. The less activity, the less self-confidence and the more self-doubts you feel, and in effect, all you do is try to drive through your life with a handbrake on, which is not the best method of travel.

It's a good thing to have brakes at hand, but it's also a good thing to be able to release them once you need to. Self-confidence is very similar—it's not about jumping into whirlpools of activities always and everywhere, but about having the ability to when you want to get somewhere or accomplish something. But before you reach this state, you will have to hustle and take massive action.

And whenever you think you are "too stressed" to act—too stressed is a lonely handicapped woman in a wheelchair, a mother of three, in debt, who has just lost her job, has very little savings, has an unpaid house mortgage and a diagnosis of cancer. Or a lone soldier under heavy fire. This is **real** stress, in terms of feeling overloaded, definitely not what you feel when you are afraid of meeting new friends, approaching a nice lady to say "hi" or going in for a job interview. Refer to this as a reference to keep your perspective straight.

EVERYTHING is a stressor

In fact, everything that requires reaction and adaptation is a stressor, so, in fact, practically everything is a perceived stressor to your body, unless you decide to stay under your bed for the rest of your life. Real, natural and lasting self-confidence is NOT about avoiding stress, nor about not feeling any stress at all (which is physically impossible, even to psychopaths!), but about learning how to deal with it, how to dismantle it in your head and how to act despite your stress.

Most of the stress we feel is easily diminished once we stop believing **that life shouldn't be stressful.**

When you believe that, that's exactly when you feel stressed the most!

In that case stress becomes a source of the feeling of failure, when it should be a reminder that you are a human being. It all comes down to how you look at your stress. If you look at it as something obvious and natural, you won't experience it so hard. **The more you try to avoid stress** (for instance, the more you stay at home every day and do nothing and never ever try new things), the more you lose your natural resistance to stress and the more stress you accumulate in your body and your subconscious mind.

The fear and anxiety that arise in us are often not even really caused by the fear of failure. The vision of failure is just a consequence resulting from a lack of action. I have learned that my level of fear and anxiety drops at the moment of taking action. This means that the **fear and anxiety don't go away only after achieving your goal, but in the exact moment of taking steps towards achieving it.** Even the circumstances that could be viewed as failure are not even close to being a source of such tremendous anxiety as that which arises when we are in the state of idleness. We are all born to survive. Evolution equipped us with fear not so we would become paralyzed, but so we would become eager to predict, estimate, analyze, travel, manufacture, evolve, etc.

How do you turn your stress into self-confidence and courage?

You have to understand that your usual level of stress is just a biological reaction characteristic for you; that's all, nothing else!

The sooner you realize and accept that it's totally natural and it's NEITHER good nor bad, it just is what it is, the sooner you will free yourself.

Or, even better, the stress can be good, if only you are willing to make it so. You have to understand that the more you fear, the braver you can be. The stronger your fear is, the stronger and higher you can rebound from it. You also need to understand that, paradoxically, usually the biggest source of stress comes from your own reaction to stress. You can choose between viewing your stress as a harmful, toxic substance, or as a source of energy and motivation, and it's entirely up to you.

For example, do you think that people doing extreme sports are devoid of any fear or emotion and dead inside? No, they are not emotionally empty, and that's the thing they always say in interviews. If you give them a closer look, you will notice that the more stressed out they were, the better results they achieved. These pros are usually extremely stressed out, but they **feel it** (**choose** to perceive it) as excitement. The more stress and cortisol they have in their systems, the better results they achieve, provided they view their stress as a booster. As many research studies conducted on soldiers and members of the Special Forces show, the people with better results during missions and special operations were the ones with higher cortisol levels and higher heart rates, those with more adrenaline and more stress in them. Also, during long and intimidating interrogations, they were much harder to break than those who were emotionally flat!

The most important factor turning stress into a useful booster is your faith that you will manage all the difficulties, consequences and obstacles. Remember that **self-trust** is simply an **act of faith** and doesn't have much to do with what has happened in the past. It's all your **decision** to make. Whenever you give yourself the right to make mistakes, knowing you will be fine anyway, it affects how you perceive stress and how you react to it.

The paradox of stress comes down to the fact that your biological reaction to stress **is your biggest asset during a stressful situation**. The key here is to understand that stress is nothing but energy, and it's up to you how to use it and where to direct it. **You can direct it either to work against you, or for you.**

Facing your fear is a radical form of self-trust. **You want to be someone who perceives his/her body and its biological processes as a resource, definitely not as something that has stopped listening to you, just because you think you "shouldn't" be stressed out and should hardly feel any stress at all**. All you can do is use this mechanism that is already inside of you. You really don't need to wait until the stress goes away to stop stressing yourself out and to start acting!

Apart from sportsmen and soldiers, there are many other types of people who flourish and bloom under the influence of stress—stunt performers, multimillionaire CEOs, actors, musicians, comedians, spies, policemen, extreme travelers. They all view stress as an occasion to grow and act more efficiently, or as something that gives their lives vivid colors. The more difficulties they face, the more work they are willing to put in, because they know all these obstacles are opportunities to prove themselves. Instead of avoiding stress, they fully engage in the role they have to play under its influence. It's a very Zen-like mindset—you simply NOTICE the stress. First you have to be aware of it without judging it, then treat it as a natural biological reaction of your system, and lastly, you need to start treating it as a resource, not an obstacle. Mind you, it isn't about being relaxed and calm. **It's about feeling stimulated.** You feel very similar things as in a "normal" state of stress, but this time the energy is aimed at your target. The truth is, the more neurotic a person is, the more hardcore of a player and achiever she/he can become. Just close your eyes, take a deep breath and feel your stress as a useful energy.

We have a tendency to prove to ourselves what we already think about ourselves and the world, so it would definitely be a good idea to think well about yourself.

Take away these points:

-The point of reference of your actions is **not the truth, but whatever works,** as Matthew Syed once put it. For example, professional sportsmen are deceiving themselves all the time. The difference is, **they deceive themselves in the direction they want**, whereas most people are deceiving themselves in the wrong direction, exactly how they were taught to do, in a direction leading them astray—"I can't do it," "It's not possible," "It's too difficult," "I'm not worthy," "I'm not good enough," "I'm not suited for this," "I won't be successful," etc. It's all about ignoring all these thoughts that contradict all your optimistic assumptions, while simultaneously focusing on good strategies, tactics and actions that will prove your optimistic assumptions.

-Talent is much less important than **how you perceive yourself**. Unless we are talking about extremely rare cases of Einstein-, Tesla- or Chopin-like talent, it doesn't mean a thing compared to hard work and dedication.

-Doublethink: the ability to profess two contradicting views at the same time, thus allowing yourself to be bipolar in order to increase your effectiveness. Let me explain.

Take a game as an example: probably every one of you has played billiards or pool at least once in your lifetime. Now, being self-confident or well-trained in this sport doesn't boil down to approaching the billiards table with the cue, hitting the billiard-ball without any preparation at all in a matter of milliseconds and counting on it falling into the right hole by itself.

Instead, you bend over the table, do your measurements and take some time to aim, as you know it's possible to miss your target, so you need at least a moment of preparation to make sure you will send the ball where you want it to go. This is the stage where you admit the thought that you might possibly fail and so you search for the best angle, tilt, position and force. But once you decide to hit the billiard-ball with the cue, you don't suddenly change the angle, your position over the table or any of these parameters and you just hit. In the moment the decision has been made, you just stick to it, instead of changing your mind every three seconds and driving the other players crazy. If you have ever watched Tiger Woods play golf, he never just approaches the ball and hits it all of a sudden, thinking he's a genius and the best golfer anyway so he doesn't have to care. He aims, calibrates, and only once he thinks he has measured everything just right, he hits the ball—then he no longer doubts.

Sometimes it's a very good idea to forget about uncomfortable and inconvenient things temporarily, only to restore your memory of them later. It's an absolutely necessary skill to have. For example, when you sit down to reflect on your life and you come to the conclusion, "I really need to change this and that," and then you analyze what exactly you should do, it wouldn't make sense not to think about the bad things in your life—you should indeed think about them and come up with the exact steps you need to take to correct your course. BUT, once you decide what to do, you switch the lever in your mind, you "hit the ball," and that's when you no longer think and overanalyze, but instead act long and consistently enough to start seeing tangible results.

-Confidence = focusing on what you want. Lack of confidence = focusing on what you don't want. And after all, you have to concentrate and focus on **something**. It's impossible not to concentrate on anything at all. Even if you suffer from ADHD, you still concentrate, just on a different thing every single moment.

Once you start being absolutely "realistic" and logical, instead of lying to yourself in a good way, you don't stand a chance of succeeding. And that's what a major part of social conditioning boils down to. Again, remember how in school no one would underline what you did right or differently from the rest in a good way, but instead every single error, eccentricity or failure of yours was underlined or crossed out in eye-hurting red?

How to be self-confident when "nothing works"

Someone once asked me how to be more active, keeping in mind that he "always fails."

This kind of bias is not a real assessment of that person's possibilities, but a certain way he thinks about himself. It's a generalization, which as a result of numerous repetitions became so automatic, passive and subconscious that it becomes a subject of no discussion at all in this person's mind.

If self-awareness, or the way we think about ourselves, is a habit, we can surely change it. You need to know how to do it and put some work into it, but it's definitely possible and worth it beyond any doubt.

When you believe, "I always fail/nothing works for me," it's really difficult to initiate any process of change and force yourself to undertake any activity, because a logical consequence of this belief is a forecast of failure, which, in effect, strengthens the sense of hopelessness associated with the thought that "nothing works" or "I always fail."
It's indeed better not to take action with such limiting beliefs. But again, how can you become self-confident

without taking action, when taking action is how you start building your self-belief and feeling of strength?

You have to divide the process into smaller stages and start changing your detrimental beliefs to helpful beliefs, supporting the change you're making and the action you take towards this change.

Throw away generalizations

Where to start?

When you take time to analyze your beliefs, pay special attention to those you are expressing with such words as "always," "never," "everything," and "nothing." These are the best places to start changing your beliefs, because life in its variability never allows anything to be "always" or "never." A person saying "I always fail" skips all the actions that have ever made them succeed or made something work.

Maybe you have often failed; maybe when something worked it wasn't exactly as you planned or as you wanted it to be; maybe the things that worked were less important than the things that failed, but it surely isn't true that "nothing worked."

If you're struggling with such beliefs, take a piece of paper and write out all the people, things and circumstances—all the things worth fighting for, things you would never agree to lose and take a moment to think how they came into your life, and what you did to bring them into or keep them in your life.

If you do this exercise honestly and truthfully, you will give yourself a chance to realize that all these things worked, even if only a little.

If you want to change your belief that "nothing's worked," start looking at your past, even your distant past, for all the moments when this statement wasn't true. Always be looking for exceptions to this rule.

Change your past

Your past is influencing the way you imagine the future.

The past filled with failures is the basis for your prediction of future failures. It's definitely more difficult to imagine future success if you've never experienced a success in a certain area in the past. In a sense, your past determines your future, because every time you start something without believing in success, you have less motivation and a lessened desire for action. When you're doing something unwillingly and reluctantly, as a rule of thumb, you don't achieve as much as it would be possible to achieve if you gave 100% of yourself.

In other words, when building on past failures, you are sabotaging your own efforts, strongly contributing to poor outcomes and gathering even more negative experiences. Does that sound like a smart thing to do?

Having said that, let's start with changing your past. You might feel confused right now—changing the past? What's that supposed to mean? What once happened, cannot be undone!

And yet, you may be surprised, but you can change your past. Or, more specifically, you can change your memory about what has happened in the past—because the past only exists in your mind, in the warehouse where your memories are stored.

Some things in this warehouse are clearly noticeable, visible at a glance—things you keep thinking about and remembering, things you tell others and yourself; these things are clear and easy to remove.

Like in any warehouse, in our memories there are some objects pushed far into a corner and covered by thick layers of dust, things we don't normally remember, but that we can also remove if we focus enough.

If you believe that so far NOTHING you have tried to accomplish has worked, it's possible that somewhere in the corners of your storage there are experiences which can work as great proof of your past successes and achievements, but you are hardly making any use of them and you don't have them on hand when you might need them. The more you remind yourself about those experiences, the more you think about and talk to yourself about them, the more vivid and important they become.

There are many people on this planet who could turn the tide of their own fortune, simply by focusing on just one particular memory, regularly nurturing and making it important.

Remember that you are the one to decide which past experiences are important to you; there's no reason to depreciate your positive experiences.

Change your understanding of past experiences

Apart from deciding to give more value to your positive past experiences, you can also do something to deal with your negative past memories. **The things you remember consist not only of facts, but also your own interpretations of what**

happened. Some experiences can be looked at from many different angles. You can also start looking for many different things in them.

In our memory, we store both an event and its past interpretation. For instance, an event that shattered your past plans might be remembered as a failure. Something that was painful and difficult for you at the time happened, so it landed in the "I failed" drawer. But today you are at least a slightly different person with a different perspective, more wisdom and many new experiences, so you can look differently at that past event.

Let me give you an example.

One woman was sexually molested by an adult when she was a little girl. Thanks to her agility and good reflexes, she managed to free herself and run away. But before she did, she felt absolutely helpless, and that's the emotion she remembered the most. Therefore, this bad experience was saved in her mind as an example of her powerlessness. As an adult, with a little help from her family and friends, she was able to note that the horrible experience can also serve as an example of a situation in which she did everything she could at that time to defend herself and escape from the hands of the degenerate, who was physically much stronger than she was. With this particular thought in mind, she will be able to gradually change the way she remembers the past experience, and start remembering it as an example of her strength, bravery and self-control.

There are also some situations in which our memories, especially the old ones, e.g., from our childhood, overlap with the interpretations and judgments of significant others, determining how we understand them, despite the fact that we've already been able to judge and interpret the situation ourselves for a long time now.

One man, as a little kid, was trying very hard to meet all the demands of the educational system. Unfortunately, he wasn't too good at doing it. His father, who probably wanted to motivate him to work harder, was always finding things that could be done better and kept criticizing him. This everyday criticism imposed on his memories in such a way that his past was full of experiences showing that no matter how hard he tried, he could never succeed or be good enough. As an adult, this man is able to change the way he remembers his past and appreciate all the things he achieved thanks to his hard work during his childhood and teenage years.

If you don't feel good enough about some area of your life, it's quite possible that you have a bunch of beliefs about yourself that inhibit your activity and act as a source of bad thoughts about yourself.

It's very important to analyze these beliefs and do everything to change them, starting from:

- Finding generalizations: the point where you stretch single facts into the size of your entire life.
- Finding exceptions: facts that prove that your generalization is not always or is almost never true.
- Nurturing and appreciating your memories and looking at them as a source of self-knowledge and self-understanding.
- Actualizing your memories; viewing them from updated, positive perspective.
- TAKING ACTION (despite uncertainty and lack of self-confidence) and setting your mind to supporting yourself instead of criticizing yourself.

REMEMBER: The thought "There's so much work to be done ahead of me!" can be a heavy load to bear; that's why you should always ask yourself about the first step: "What can I do TODAY, before the sun sets, to bring myself even a little bit closer to my goal?"

Your relation with yourself

The very basis of self-confidence is self-acceptance. It's the most crucial and important thing. You have to realize all of your shortcomings, and once you do, accept them. You need to appreciate your value. You are a unique human being and you deserve to feel great about yourself.

If you want to know what I mean, please try this exercise: think of all the things that you are proud of and write them down on a piece of paper. Think about everything there is; for example, maybe you have great friends, outstanding passions, or a nice place to live, or maybe you just like your hair. The fact that you're reading this book means that you are motivated to change and you're actually doing something to improve your situation, so you have another good reason to be proud of yourself! The best idea is to write these things out—as many of them as you can. **Everyone can write out at least 35 things they're proud of!** This way you will strengthen your belief in your self-worth.

Do it now and write it down in your "confidence notebook." If you already made a list in the exercise in which I asked you to think about which positive attributes and traits you could start exposing and developing more, you should expand on that list now. Additionally, apart from character traits, aspects of your personality and previous successes, you should also write down all the simple things that make you happy in your current situation. These things could be as trivial as liking your neighbors or the city you live in, having a cool mother-in-law, and so on.

You can also do the same in a computer file, but it's important to write it down by hand first! Keep it and **keep making it bigger and bigger**, every time you come up with a new thing you are proud of or like about yourself!

Self-confident beliefs

Once you know your pros, it's time to change your beliefs. The biggest ill of our society is the question, **"What will others think?"** You may be thinking, "Nah, that's not me!" But please, stop reading for a moment and really think about **how many times you have done something not in your best interests, just because someone else could have thought something bad or strange about you?** It's ridiculous that so many people allow the fear of other people's opinions to control their lives.

You have to make a decision—either you will be the one to make decisions about your life, or you will accept the fact that others will decide for you. Let people think what they want to think, what difference does it make? **Unless you want to look back at your life in a few years' time and notice that your life is a result of the potential thoughts and opinions of others.** I don't know about you, but I want to be the one to decide about my own life and fate.

Isn't it sick to give up on things that you truly desire just because, according to you, someone **may** think badly about you (even though in most cases, **nothing like that will even happen,** as most people don't really give a crap about what other people do)?

In my work with people who lack confidence, the most crucial, important and difficult thing to do is to change their beliefs such as "People will think I'm a weirdo," "People will laugh at me," "What will my family think?," etc. These beliefs are great foundations for stress, which shows up just when you want to start doing something meaningful with your life. Get rid of them and you will truly progress and take a big, big step forward!

A very wise woman, Eleanor Roosevelt, famously once said, "No one can make you feel inferior without your consent." Truly dwell on the wisdom of that philosophical statement for a moment. You might be thinking, "Wait, what? People make me feel inferior all the time, and I sure as hell am not letting them do it—it just happens!" However, if you deeply contemplate the thought, you will grow to learn its powerful truth: you may receive negativity from others, but only you willingly give up the authority that allows them to make you feel inferior about yourself.

Now, granted, certainly no one wants to become so hardened that anything negative said towards them is dismissed with the thoughts, "I refuse to feel inferior!" and "I refuse to dwell on the negativity!" A crucial part of self-growth is being open to true, sincere, constructive criticism. So if you receive negative input from someone, think to yourself, "What can I learn from this? Is this a moment when I can recognize a semblance of truth and find an area within myself to improve upon? Or is this something that I should dismiss because it was said in ignorance and pettiness, and is it damaging and not conducive to self-growth?" Take the truth, even if it is negative, and turn it around into a positive. The benefits of this are two-fold: you are NOT allowing anyone to MAKE you feel inferior about yourself, and you are still welcoming any opportunity to learn about yourself and to perhaps become aware of a shortcoming that you truly do want to improve upon. Later in this book I will show you a great exercise that will help you deal with other people's criticism and harshness.

Paradoxically and funnily enough, when you say what's on your mind and act directly, not worrying about anyone's opinion, **that's exactly when you gain other people's respect.** That's when people see that you are self-confident and that they should treat you right. So keep this in mind and never forget it—what other people think of you and your actions DOESN'T MATTER (unless you're ruining your neighbors' cars with a baseball bat, throwing chewed bubble gum at your manager's kids or ruining your date's favorite carpet by making mandalas out of crushed candy... Then, I agree, it might matter to some degree). You're the only person to decide about the quality of your life.

Below you will find **beliefs that strongly support your confidence and self-esteem**. Take them as thought bricks to build your mindset with, and try each one of them in real life.

Here's the next mission for you: For a next couple of days, treat the beliefs listed below as though they were 100% real at all times. Observe how your thoughts and reactions change when you look at the world through other lenses, and take notes!

The best idea would be to write these beliefs down on small cards and spend one day with each of them at a time. You could take the card out of your pocket when you're waiting in traffic, at the bus stop, or in the elevator or are almost asleep at boring lectures. Look at them several times a day and reflect on them, imagining how your life would look if you felt they were always 100% true and if you always acted on them.

Changing your beliefs is a very important part of working on your confidence.

Here they are:

-<u>No matter what happens, I WILL handle it!</u>

-There are no defeats and failures, just feedback.

-I'm alright.

-I'm valuable and unique.

-No criticism says anything about me as a person, just about my actions and behaviors, which I can change.

- Critics criticize to feel better in their own skin.
- I don't have to fulfill other people's expectations if I don't want to.
- Saying "no" to others is natural and okay with me.

-The idealized image of myself I used to wear was an illusion.

- I shouldn't: I want. (You don't *have* to do anything at all with your life; the right mindset is not "I SHOULD do it" but "I WANT to do it.)
- I fully accept myself as I am right now.
- My flaws are an integral part of my life and I fully accept them.

-Underneath my masks and beliefs there's a diamond I have always been.

- Self-confidence is always dependent on the context.
- I'm not the mask I wear or the social roles I play.
- Natural self-confidence is not about climbing walls, but realizing they don't really exist.

-I'm fully responsible for the emotions I feel.

- My system has the ability to feel calm and peaceful. The stress I occasionally feel is natural and helpful to me.
- I'm completely safe at all times and everywhere.
- I'm constantly actualizing my thinking so it stays relevant to reality.

-The more experiences I gain, the safer I feel.

- I'm consequently broadening my comfort zone.
- Every new challenge = a gain in comfort in a new area of life.
- What else do I want to experience in my life?

-Inside of me, I have all the resources I will ever need.

- It's OK not to know something.
- People are open to new relations.
- I'm the one to decide how other people's thoughts and opinions about me affect me.

-I'm not a navel of the universe. People always focus on their own lives.

- People have their own problems and don't feel the need to assess me all the time.
- I concentrate on and listen to what other people have to say.

- I don't need other people's opinion to accept myself and to choose for myself.

  -All people in the world are equal as human beings and I should stay humble no matter how far I get in my life.

- Nothing external builds my self-esteem.
- I've been unconditionally valuable since the day I was born.
- What else makes me valuable?

  -Every thought I choose to think influences how I feel in a given moment and in my life in general.

- I care for my internal representations, so they support my self-confidence.
- Day by day, I'm becoming better at controlling my emotions.

Read these beliefs every single day until they become an integral part of yourself. They are golden.

Moreover, be sure to do this: For every single one of these beliefs, write down (on a piece of paper, in your "confidence notebook," not in an electronic device) at least three logical arguments to back them up, apart from the bullet points below each of them.

Find reasons why they are true. You can come up with a short story or an example from your own life or a belief you already have. For the belief "No matter what happens, I will handle it" you have to write down ten arguments backing it up.

This is your homework. Take it seriously and take action.

Getting out of your comfort zone

The mythical "comfort zone" so often talked about is nothing but the range of behaviors and situations in your life in which you feel comfortable, safe and secure. All the things outside of your comfort zone make you feel stressed and insecure. For example, approaching strange people at parties to make friends with them might be outside your comfort zone, whereas asking them for the time might be within your comfort zone.

It all comes down to constantly expanding your comfort zone **and incorporating new areas of your life into it.** When some behavior, action or situation is a part of your comfort zone, it will never make you feared or stressful. How do you expand your comfort zone? Only by doing things that are outside of its borders.

Only when you discover that your fears were unfounded and unnecessary will they vanish forever. So every single day you should be doing things that scare you or used to scare you before.

Let me give you a few examples. Go down the street and smile at strangers. When on a bus, sing your favorite song, clearly and visibly moving your lips. Go to a part of your city where you've never been before (unless it's a place you shouldn't be going without a machine gun and grenade launcher). Talk to strangers. Ask them how to get somewhere or for their opinion on something. Go through the supermarket with your left hand raised and keep it that way. Go to a club alone and meet people. Or jump into a fountain. Remember that all of your fears are primitive and primal. You are absolutely safe and just need to rewire your brain and tell it, "Dude, come on, take a look around, it's 2016 already! We don't live in caves anymore!" enough times that it finally gets it.

When we make a decision and take action, our current situation (and hence, various possible risks) becomes more real and clearer. It becomes more defined. And what's more defined is never as terrifying as something we can't describe or can't clearly see and define. This phenomenon is easily observed if you watch horror films—we feel the most tension in those parts of the movie when something gets closer and closer, the floor creaks, the window shutter slams into the window frame and we can sense that there's SOMETHING hiding in the dark. That's when we fear the most. But once this "something" materializes into a shape of some kind, even as the most obnoxious monster or vampire, the tension decreases. No zombie or mummy in any movie will ever induce such fear as we feel when we don't know what's lurking around the corner. Once you see it—the fun is over.

The same effect applies to real life, when we are so afraid that something might happen that we don't even try to think about what that "something" might really be or whether it can really happen. We stop at the thought that something will be scary and we become petrified. We pause our "internal horror film" in the exact moment of the greatest tension, and then we rewind it to the beginning. A good medicine for our fear is often simply to watch "the movie" to the end.

I guess you already know what it's about. Going on "missions" is the best and fastest way to boost your confidence. Once you start doing them, your comfort zone will increase quickly and for good, and your confidence will follow. This is true in all areas of your life. Do you want to be more self-confident during public speeches? Give as many public speeches as you can, and so on. Thanks to such a mindset you will start feeling much better in all kinds of life situations. Doing all these things will make you feel as good as possible, absolutely cool and self-confident.

Take your "confidence notebook" and write out all of the missions you will be doing during the coming week. One mission a day, seven days straight—no breaks. Start with the easiest things (e.g., smiling at strangers on the streets), gradually progressing to more and more difficult missions. You will see that they will all be stressful only at the beginning. After only a short time, you will feel more self-confident. Some time ago, after a seminar I was taking part in, we hit the streets with the attendees and started doing things that would be considered socially "strange" by most people. We would approach people and start asking them silly (not disrespectful, but uncommon) questions, and even ended up taking a shower in the city fountain. After no longer than a single hour of having this type of fun, the majority of us gained the courage to break the ice and started feeling about 200% more confident in further social interactions.

How to be self-confident in professional relations

Have you ever felt that during conversations with people much higher on the "social ladder" than yourself, your confidence takes a deep dive down and you find yourself shaky, with your legs trembling? How do you feel more self-confident and relaxed in these situations?

Again, it's mainly about frame of mind. You need to focus on the fact that the social hierarchy that places them above you was artificially created by our society. It's an abstraction, a construction. Apart from their perceived value and possibly much higher incomes, they are normal human beings, just like you and me. When you're overly stressed, it's harder to create a good relation with someone and access the resources we need in such situations, such as lack of self-judgments, relaxed body posture, accurate responses, etc. These are four beliefs that are the most detrimental:

1. This person has authority/power over me.
2. This person can decide what happens to me.
3. I'm not qualified enough to talk to this person.
4. I'll probably say something worthless or dumb.

These beliefs are not real. You need to realize the truth in order to feel relaxed in these situations.

The first two beliefs/situations might be true, but only in professional situations. Your boss can fire you, but it doesn't affect your entire life (you were smart enough to get this job; you could find another) and you need to narrow your belief to the professional context only. Even if you do get fired, you are a free person, after all, you are free to make decisions about your own life.

The last two beliefs are not truthful and are not in accordance with reality. You need to understand that and work on them. You HAVE alternatives, you can think differently and look at the situation differently, and in reality YOU ARE THE ONE TO CHOOSE what to think about it.

How do you do it? You need to apply the so called "thought strategies." These are strategies and ways of thinking about what a given person might think about you, how they might judge you or how they might react to a potential blunder or a mistake resulting from you being stressed out during a given situation. The main problem lies in the fact that the majority of people only focus on a small range of possible things a given person might think about them. They only take a small part of the whole truth into consideration, for example, "My boss will think I'm incompetent," and then they repeat it again and again in their minds, falling into a loop.

They never think about what a given person might have thought about them previously and how it might affect their view of the recent setback, or what the person will think one hour, a few days or a week later. This type of thinking generates a feeling of extreme stress, which fucks them up. They become shattered, paralyzed and even less intelligent, unless they stop repeating this dumb loop. This makes it hard for them to be themselves and use the resources they already have.

Let me now show you an exercise that might be very helpful in solving this particular problem. It helps you create and see a longer timeline, thanks to which you stop obsessing and stumbling over a small piece of reality, a tiny segment of a timeline. Moreover, it helps you extend your useless, scary thoughts to the point of the absurd, which helps a ton and makes things much easier.

This technique is helpful for two reasons: first of all, you set up an entirely new extreme limit to what you tend to think or imagine. For example, if you fear your

CEO will think that you are worthless and you suck, you start imagining the absolute, extreme limit of what might happen, so it becomes silly and funny. This way, the thought that used to haunt you is now making you laugh. It ceases to be so terrible and is not a burden anymore. Second of all, while creating such ridiculous absurdities in your head, you also create positive emotions, which anchor (emotionally connect) to your fearful thoughts, so the thoughts become positive, as well, or neutral. Either way, you start feeling relaxed and free, exactly what you need if you want to have good conversations with people with a higher social status.

Ok, here's how to do the exercise. In order to break a persistent mental pattern, create an absurdity, and to escape the annoying loop, you can imagine, for instance, the following things:

1. After talking to you, your boss feels so scandalized that he feels the need to show the entire world the bitter truth about you. So he designs flyers with you wearing an orange prison suit and holding a banner with "WANTED!" written on it in big type, along with a detailed description of your incompetent behavior. Then he walks around town with a silly backpack and hands the flyers to people on the streets and on buses

and to little kids in kindergarten classes. Then he doesn't sleep at night, because he's friending and talking to all of your friends on Facebook, telling them how horrible you are and how they should stop hanging out with you. Then he calls your parents and shouts at them about how they failed in raising you properly, then he buys big banners in the city center with ads showing you making stupid faces or picking your nose and a message, "AVOID THIS DUMB MUFF AT ALL COSTS!!!," etc.

2. Your boss or manager is so furious after meeting with you that his face goes all red, he starts screaming, demolishes his whole office with a baseball bat, and throws the computers and all of his things through the closed window, then falls on his knees and starts pulling his hair out, crying like a little baby, etc.

3. He calls the police, the FBI and the army, records a movie about you and shows it in cinemas worldwide, then tries to schedule a meeting with the president or prime minister to tell them how disastrous you were and how you should be banned from your country, and so on.

Let your mind wander off and have fun with the process. Make yourself laugh. It's about creating a thought so absurd, ridiculous and silly, your brain will start rewiring the reactions that used to appear. This

Zen-like technique breaks the loop and makes you play with your fear, transforming it into a joke and an amusement. After all this, when you really meet the people you were previously afraid of, you will notice that your reactions are easier and much more relaxed.

A few more important words about self-confidence and the proper mindset

After having read this part, you now know everything you need to know and you have all the required foundations to kickstart your personal transformation journey. However, before we proceed to the healthy self-esteem part, I need to tell you something else.

In life, the things we are afraid of, all the things that we think that "might happen," are usually much easier to cope with than we imagine they will be, if they even happen at all. The fright I felt at the mere thought of quitting my job, sending my hard-earned money abroad to a company that could theoretically screw me, ending a relationship I felt trapped in, etc., was always much worse than what I felt after or while doing these things. And it's not just me; I know from experience that's how it usually is in everyone's life.

However, with things we are excited about or want to achieve, we usually underestimate the amount of hard work we need to put in, what we will have to sacrifice to get there and how many obstacles there will be for us to overcome. Take the gym, for example. Many people see all those bald, predatory-looking, extremely muscular guys and say things like, "Phew! This is so simple and primitive! You just go there, lift the stupid weights and eat lots of food! This is stupid!"

The joke starts when someone like that actually joins the gym, instead of just standing in front of the pond and telling fish how to swim. It quickly becomes apparent how much knowledge about the human body, physical exercise, dieting, healthy supplements and even biochemistry is required, not to mention the discipline and all the sacrifices needed.

These people often say things along the lines of, "Oh! I've been exercising for one month now and still I don't see any results! I'm still fat! This is stupid! All these guys are cheating and taking steroids!" They don't understand how much self-education, humility, patience, perseverance and time is needed in order to master each given area of live. Having said that, if you read all the books about self-confidence and self-esteem in the world, but don't keep that simple truth in mind, you will go nowhere.

You might need a mentor or a trainer who will teach you a certain life skill and make you accountable. And then you have to STICK TO THE PLAN. Don't be another damn fool bringing people down, because "I've already tried this two times; each time I put a month of my life into this and I still don't see any results!! The gym doesn't work; you need steroids! Owning businesses don't work; it's all a capitalist scam! You have to go to a normal job! You can't meet people on the street and in clubs; it's not normal!" Oh! How moving; it's truly been emotional. May I hand you a tissue? Stop whining, stick to it, commit and go for it and you **will** see the results. It's really as simple as that. Repetition, repetition, repetition. You can't be self-confident until a new skill is not new anymore. How many of you bail after your first failure? You know how many publishers J.K Rowling was rejected by? Twelve! Remember how many failed light bulbs Edison built? Hundreds! Do what you have to do and don't accept "no" for an answer. It will be much easier if you surround yourself with people going the same direction.

Now, I've also noticed that far too many people have the fatal mechanism of bringing themselves down. For example, a total nerd, who has never had a single girlfriend because video games were his only friends for the past two decades, finds out that it might be possible to meet nice girls on the street and in clubs without making a frustrated and weird bum out of himself. So he starts. Obviously, all the girls ignore him because he's stressed out and acts like an alien or a total geek. So instead of thinking, "Yeah, I was strong enough to quit computer games, start improving my looks and start learning how to talk to real people and be a fun guy," he thinks, "Oh no! I'm so pathetic! I'm so stupid! All the girls ignore me! This is going nowhere I'm going back to my PC where I spent the past 20 years! My PC always loves me!" The same goes for the gym—"Two month of exercising, half an hour a day, three times a week and after 15 years of eating total junk and watching TV I'm still a fat ass! How is that even possible?!," it goes for business—"I've been learning about this for three months now; I've even bought a stamper, installed Google Chrome and changed my wallpaper to a more serious one, and still I didn't make any sales! The world is unfair! SELF-EMPLOYMENT IS A SCAM! It's unrealistic! I'll go to Mum and start wiping my tears on her apron!"— ... and so on. Seriously though, DON'T FALL INTO THIS TRAP. The journey is long. The journey is demanding. Most people on this planet live crappy lives, because they don't want to accept this simple fact. If you want to really become decent as something, you need to put in lots of time and energy. Stop believing in reaping without sowing beforehand. So start today and keep that in mind.

You have to enjoy the process. **You have to do everything you can to grow to like it. If you're going to the gym, do anything it takes to fall in love with it. Look for all the positive things it gives you. Do everything you can to fall in love with your diet.** Always appreciate what you do and do everything you can to enjoy the activities you're trying to start doing! Most people are not even smart and strong enough to start reading self-dev books, or specialist, niche-oriented books (e.g., aerospace engineering 101, etc.), not to mention face their fear. **So if you have already started, you are WAY ahead of 99% of all other people! Don't mess it up by bringing yourself down. Enjoy it!** Every single day brings you closer to your goal, even if it's just one millimeter a day. You **are** getting there! Make your new journey your lifestyle. Don't treat going to gym, meeting new people, learning how to give public speeches, starting your own business or learning how to code software with the lame mindset, "I will do this for six months and then slack off, just enjoying the results." It will go on and on; the perfect sweet point is usually when you don't ever want to stop, when you don't want to lie on a Caribbean beach for five months doing nothing. You want to continue on your journey of getting better. Sometimes you might feel that a particular area of your life is mastered enough and focus more on other aspects, but the self-growth should never stop. That's where real happiness comes from, you will see! So—enjoy what you do, appreciate your strength and your perseverance, enjoy every single small step. Enjoy all of your failures, as they only mean that **you had enough courage to start, whereas most people are lazy asses and don't even care to begin changing anything at all.** Be grateful for all the possibilities in your life; accept stagnations and even the fact that sometimes you might find yourself unwillingly taking a step backward.

Always look for people who are already great at what you do, people you can learn from. Don't beat yourself up on that journey! You will be continuing it for many years, or hopefully your entire life, as there are hardly any limits to self-development in any given area. You can always be better at something. **It's addictive, and it's the best addiction you could have!**

Even more ideas on how to become self-confident

There are many different ways to develop your self-confidence. Below I describe some of them. Depending on where you are in your life right now, you might need all of these ways, or just some of them.

I'm not giving you fixed solutions, but rather general directions. I want to show you a full picture, a map that tells you how you can work on your self-confidence. You don't necessarily need all of these ideas, but I'm sure you will find what you are looking for. After you're done reading, ask yourself, "What do I need the most?" Then make a decision and give all your attention and focus to developing the chosen area.

1. Take good care of yourself. Treat yourself as someone important and valuable. Do you know how good friends treat one another? With kindness, trust, respect, support, motivation, and understanding.

Treat yourself exactly the same way. Take care of yourself also in the more practical understanding of this term—take care of your needs, such as the need to have fun, take a good rest, spend time with loved ones, enjoy healthy nutrition, play sports, etc.

2. Quit basing your self-esteem on external factors (like what others think about you, what grades you have in school, how much you earn, how many material possessions you own, how many friends you have, how you look). Instead, support your self-esteem with internal factors (like your moral system and values, what's important to you, who you want to become, what your goals are, what are your life's work and personal mission on this planet). Don't attach your self-esteem to something that doesn't belong to you, because then it can collapse at any moment. You will read more about this in Part III of this book.

3. Constantly build your feeling of self-worth. Always focus on moments in your life when you accomplish something, i.e., one of your goals, even the tiniest one. Create the already-mentioned list of traits and events that prove your value. Strengthen and support yourself. Write down your successes and constantly remind yourself of them. Build a strong belief that you are a valuable person and LEARN how to appreciate yourself. It's a HABIT, not an inborn trait.

4. Work on accepting your own flaws and imperfections. We all have them but we don't usually like them. To learn self-acceptance you have to observe yourself, your behaviors, thoughts and emotions. It's funny how much time in life we spend learning about many different things, but how rarely we... learn about ourselves. So today start learning about yourself! Investigate why you act one way and not another. What is the source of your behaviors and emotions? What thoughts, beliefs and emotions underlie your actions? Understand yourself and you will start being much more forgiving to yourself. It's also very important to realize that the lack of self-acceptance is not a good motivator and not a good stimulus to change (contrary to the popular and wrong belief, "If I accept myself, I will stop caring about self-development and changing my life and hence won't change anything for the better"), but is instead the strongest brake on and the biggest obstacle to self-development and living life to the fullest. Learn how to have a distance from yourself and laugh at your flaws. You will read more about this topic in the last part of this book where I will show you many practical and effective exercises.

"I laugh at myself. I don't take myself completely seriously.
I think that's another quality that people have to hold on to... you have to laugh, especially at yourself." - Madonna

5. Increase your competence. When I first started my work as a guy helping people with their problems, without any previous experience, I felt insecure. Now, after a few years, thanks to the competence I have gained, I feel secure and free in my work. Competence is the basis of self-confidence in relation to some areas of life. If you lack self-confidence in human relations, take a few months to explore the topic and learn about communication skills and human relations from A to Z.

This chapter can serve you as a simple, general map, based on which you can start building your further education and self-development in self-confidence. Full and complete education about how our minds work in the context of self-esteem and self-confidence is the best way to build a natural foundation for lasting confidence.

One last thing.

Once you start your journey and begin to see progress, find three contexts in which you will be hard to throw off the scent because you know you are good in them, so every time someone says, "I'm better than you," you will know it's not true, or is at least far-fetched. Know the areas in which you are better than most people and lead the conversation in those directions.

You can make a list of what you're afraid people might potentially say about you. Then find three examples of situations when you really acted or behaved so. So, if someone said you're average, you could think about situations in which you were average indeed (e.g., on your math tests, if you are not a math guy, or... when just sitting on a toilet like everybody else), but then it will be your own opinion, not someone else's.

Then find three counterarguments, situations in which you behaved in a special or outstanding way. Always build a "me" that is set on real, tangible and undeniable foundations and evidence.

Avoid arrogance, but also avoid false modesty, as we've been told that we should never brag. Why not? If someone has earned it, if, according to solid facts, that person really deserves praise, then it's a good thing and others should be inspired by it.

If they are not... well, that's their problem.

Finally, there's something to think about, if you think you are in a really bad place in life—just theoretically, as in reality it's not possible, but what if everything you've ever done was wrong?

What if from now on you started doing everything the other way around? What if you wrote down your ways of acting and seeing things and broke them down into single cells--then thought about how your life would look if you turned some of these cells upside down? Give it a thought. Maybe you will realize it wouldn't be better that way. Maybe you will consider doing some things differently. Stretch your mind a little bit.

PART III: SELF-ESTEEM

So you have covered the self-confidence part of the book. I told you about the right mindset, the way to go about things, practical steps to take and exercises to do, but there's much more. Natural self-confidence and healthy self-esteem go hand in hand. The latter is required if you want to maintain your self-confidence at a high level, avoiding emotional highs and lows. It's also necessary to stay emotionally healthy and in great relationships with other people. Let's go even deeper into the rabbit hole and see where it goes!

In psychology, self-esteem is described as a general, subjective evaluation of our own value and our personality, but it's also about our general approach to ourselves: our relationship with ourselves. It can be either positive or negative. Self-esteem includes different beliefs about ourselves, including assessment of our own behaviors, emotions, attitudes, appearance, etc. In his book *Psychology and Life*, Philip Zimbardo defines self-esteem as a generalized assessment of "'self."

Psychotherapist Nathaniel Branden defines self-esteem as the "experience of being competent in being able to cope with the basic challenges of life and deserving happiness."

"Low self-esteem is like driving through life with your hand-brake on." – Maxwell Maltz

When it's too low, it results in a lack of confidence and a feeling of low self-worth. People with such a mindset perceive themselves as inferior to others (based on different criteria such as looks, social status, income or IQ) and see themselves as less valuable than they really are, which makes them feel bad, when they are alone or around other people. These people characteristically hold many beliefs that start with "I should/I should have": "I should be smarter," "I should be more social," "I should care less about other people," "I should earn more," etc. People with low self-esteem are very harsh self-critics; they often punish themselves and think they don't deserve much from life.

When one's self-esteem is too high, on the other hand, it results in feelings of exaltation and arrogance. It's just an apparent confidence—not a genuine one. These people also operate on the scheme of "the best" and "the worst," frequently oscillating between these two, but rarely anywhere in the middle. These people have the strong belief that they are superior. They attribute to themselves qualities they don't really have, or think they can do things they really can't do. Having biased opinion of themselves, they appear more confident than people with lower opinions about themselves, but are still consumed by fear—because in every situation there's always the risk of someone better than them showing up. And in situations when this "risk" comes to fruition, a defense mechanism in the form of arrogance or even aggression is activated.

So… how do you evaluate yourself in a healthy way?

Healthy self-esteem is a state in which we know ourselves well and feel great "in our skins," along with all the advantages and disadvantages that we have. The way a person with natural and healthy self-esteem perceives the world can be represented by these two sentences:

"I know my flaws and I accept them. I know my strengths and I appreciate them."

When our self-esteem is healthy, in relationships with others, we quit the "better/worse" scheme and finally, we become aware of the fact that everyone is different, but we are all "equal" in this uniqueness. There are no better and worse people as such, it's just that because of many different variables and circumstances, some people have developed certain character traits or certain skillsets better than others.

"There is overwhelming evidence that the higher the level of self-esteem, the more likely one will be to treat others with respect, kindness, and generosity." – Nathaniel Branden

The "recipe for self-esteem"

Obviously, healthy self-esteem is an extraordinarily important thing to have. You can't achieve any real success in life without it. If you ask a psychologist where it comes from, they will certainly reply that it's formed during early childhood, based on relationships between the kid and their family members, or other people important to the kid. Unfortunately, parents play a big role here. I say "unfortunately" because perfection is something as rare as unicorns in our world (if it's possible at all), and issues that result from our upbringing are often hard to change in adult life. However, you have to remember that healthy self-esteem is not something given to us once and forever! If it's high, it can fall down; if it's small, it can grow, depending on circumstances and what we do in our lives. So if your childhood didn't give you very many positive experiences to enable you to feel good and confident about yourself, know that nothing is lost yet. You can change it, starting today!

Non-effective ways of building self-esteem

It's really hard to build healthy self-esteem just by making the decision to start liking and appreciating yourself and putting in minimal effort. It won't help much to merely repeat affirmations, not least because if you have very low self-esteem, you won't believe in these positive sentences about yourself in your default state of consciousness (although a professional hypnotherapist/psychotherapist might help).

The advice to look in the mirror and tell yourself, "I love you" might really help or even do wonders if your level of self-esteem is at least somewhat healthy, but for people who really hate themselves it could be misguided—such a person might not be able to do that, because of the pain that looking at themselves with a total lack of acceptance involves. It might work in some cases, but do nothing in others.

You also won't be able to build healthy self-esteem based on other people's acceptance, and often it also won't be possible or smart to build it solely on your achievements and social advancements. If, according to you, your value depends on other people's acceptance or on succeeding at something, then you're making your entire self-esteem dependent on external circumstances. In doing so you're just reinforcing your fear of criticism and failure. When scared, you withdraw - you stop taking action (because you think you might get criticized, rejected etc.) and therefore lower your self-esteem.

Note that typical, intuitive methods of building self-esteem usually lead in the opposite direction than desired, as you are making yourself weaker instead of stronger.

Effective ways of building self-esteem

Please notice that we're now talking about the subjective FEELING of your own worth, not about your objective worth as a person. We're talking about the importance of what you feel, not your value seen through the eyes of others. If we have that inner sense in mind, then it's certain that the road to self-esteem leads directly inside you—so that almost nothing external will be able to build or ruin it.

Of course, there are some circumstances in which it's easier to maintain our self-esteem, and others in which it's much harder to do. The external world influences us—when a confident person is subject to massive criticism, they can start having doubts, but still, it takes an inner change to rebuild the feeling of self-esteem, not an external change. That's why in such situations it doesn't make sense to get into discussions with the critics and it's much better to get into a discussion with yourself. The better self-esteem you have, the more easily you will overcome difficult circumstances.

You can use the metaphor of sailing on the sea—the bigger and better-equipped your yacht is, the bigger a storm you can endure and the further you will get. If you are sailing in a barrel equipped with a single oar, it will certainly be much harder to sail through stormy waters than in a modern sailing boat. Cultivation of self-esteem is just like building a good sailing boat.

If you got self-esteem as a gift from your parents, that's nice. If you didn't, no worries—just build it yourself. **You need these six tools:**

1. Self-awareness,

2. Self-acceptance,

3. Assertiveness,

4. Proactiveness,

5. Responsibility,

6. Cohesion.

That's all you need.

Six pillars of healthy self-esteem

Self-awareness

You can't value something you know nothing about. To be able to rate something, you have to have a wide knowledge about the item, you have to know what it's for, what it's made of, what can be done with it, etc.

When you want to evaluate yourself, you need to **know yourself**—know what you really want, what drives you, why you do what you do, what your strong and weak sides are, how you can use them, etc. If you don't know what your motives are, if you do things and don't know why, if you're running away from self-awareness, addicting yourself to chemistry or certain mindless behaviors, if you live without inner involvement and your focus is not to feel much—you can't know your own value and thus you can't build healthy self-esteem.

Goal no. 1: Embark on a mission to truly get to know yourself, starting from learning about yourself, not from judging yourself.

Tip: You can start by taking a 16-personalities type test online, for free. For example, on this website (it takes about ten minutes):

http://www.16personalities.com/

Note that the test result is not a mirror or an absolute, and I deeply believe that personality is something you actively MAKE; it's flexible to a great extent; you can change it throughout your life; it's just the system that you've built so far, but this test can be an informative road sign on your way.

According to this test, I'm supposed to be an ENTJ personality type and I must admit this is a very accurate overall description of the traits, strengths and weaknesses I've been showing since early childhood.

Also, the technique of everyday questions is a fantastic and simple tool that allows you to deepen your self-awareness. It helps you take a closer look at important moments in your life. For instance, if you want to know if you are really happy in a relationship, you could, for a chosen period of time, write down how happy you feel with your partner every day (on a scale of 1 to 10) and which event affected your happiness the most. Thanks to this you will be able to consciously assess the quality of your relationship. It could also inspire you to take better care of your relationship.

You can apply everyday questions to every single aspect of your life that you want to be more aware of. It's especially helpful to assess situations in which you often feel a lack of satisfaction. My favorite questions are, "For what am I grateful right now?," "What made me happy today?," and "What do I need now?"

And lastly—the best tool to get to REALLY know yourself and understand your reactions, behaviors, needs and motives is everyday meditation. Twenty minutes a day, every day, is enough. Without meditation and mindfulness, you will have a really hard time getting to know yourself well.

Self-acceptance

Learning about and getting to really know yourself is the first step. The second step is to accept what you have learned. Self-acceptance is a recognition and appreciation of who you really are, even if the image that emerges from the self-awareness is not too beautiful. If you find a gemstone on a dirty road, you won't be amazed immediately. It's not really attractive, seemingly just a piece of rock—but if you throw it away you will never gain what you would have gained if you washed it, polished it and gave it a beautiful shape. If you throw yourself away today, then you will keep throwing yourself away in the future. If you accept yourself today, you can evolve and change in the future. The road to positive change leads through acceptance—even acceptance of the fact that your level of self-esteem is low and it doesn't make you feel too confident.

Self-acceptance is a full approval of who you are, i.e., of all the emotions that you feel, of all of your needs, desires, dreams, of how you decide to behave, of who you decide to hang out with or ignore and decide what to do and what to avoid.

One important thing I should mention here is satisfaction. It works like an internal barometer showing how much you accept yourself. Maybe you are trying really hard, but still feeling dissatisfied; you feel you are not doing enough, or you think you could've done something better. The road to perfectionism is short, and the road to fulfillment is long. I know people who do colossal work on a daily basis, but still feel it's not enough to make them satisfied with themselves. And yet there's another world available—one seen through the eyes of a satisfied person, who thinks, "What I do and how I do it is good enough. I know how to appreciate my efforts and my energy. Even if something's not going too well, I see how much I give and how much action I take and I'm grateful to myself for all that." In my opinion, the feeling of dissatisfaction is a form of self-punishment for what you do and how you are. And like the psychologist Milton Ericsson, I deeply believe that everyone gives as much of themselves as they can in a certain moment and if they could give themselves more, they would surely do it. If you try as hard as you can, don't punish yourself! If you take action and think long-term, everything you do is just perfect at this stage and it couldn't be better given your present state, skills and experience.

Keeping a satisfaction journal will help you in self-diagnosis and better awareness of how much you experience satisfaction and how often. During the next month, every single day write down how satisfied you felt on a scale from one to ten (where one means not at all, and ten means fully satisfied). Also write down what contributed the most to the feeling of satisfaction with yourself. (It will help you discover what's most important to you in your life, what really counts and makes sense.)

After that month, decide if your current situation satisfies you. If the answer is negative, come up with measurable and attainable goals in the sphere that dissatisfies you.

Also, I have homework for you to do now.

First of all, write down all of the failures you think were important in your life and have influenced your overall confidence. Once you're done, write down all the good things that resulted from these failures happening to you. Write down all the things that you've learned from them, all the people you've met, all the good situations that you've encountered, all the places you've been to instead of being somewhere else, how the failures made you stronger and wiser person. Every single failure is a building material, a road sign on a crossroads, a pointer—it GIVES YOU self-confidence in some area and teaches you something important about your life. Write down at least three things you have learned thanks to all of these failures!

Secondly, write down all of the flaws and shortcomings you think you have, all of your negative aspects. This can be a character trait or an aspect of your appearance, a desire to which you feel resistance or a negative emotion you're experiencing. Previously in the book I asked you to do a similar exercise and write out everything you think is a flaw in yourself, so if you already did the exercise, you can now use it as a reference for this one.

Then, below each one, write down three ways to laugh at this flaw. Imagine contexts in which each one of these flaws could be funny to you. Write these down. Moreover, think about ways you can make yourself laugh by distancing yourself from your own imperfections.

Now think about the benefits you have obtain from feeling so, looking so, behaving or acting like that; about contexts in life in which this flaw could be useful and helpful. Write down five of them, at least! Then, think of the benefits other people might obtain from you feeling so, behaving or acting in a certain way. What have you discovered? How do you feel when you look at yourself this way? Once you accept an aspect of yourself that you've so far disavowed or resisted, then you can change it. But change doesn't happen when you fight with part of yourself; it happens only when you immerse this part of yourself in love.

Once you're done, perform the process described below:

Remember a moment in your life when you accepted something or someone fully. It doesn't matter what the subject of acceptance was, but it's important to choose a situation in which you really, fully felt the state of acceptance. Maybe someone asked you for permission to do something and you agreed, knowing that it was a really good idea. Maybe you accepted someone's positive behavior. Find such a memory.

Close your eyes and remember that situation very thoroughly and as vividly as possible. Once you start feeling the emotion of acceptance, locate it in your body. Where do you feel this emotion? Once you know answer to this question, think about the color and shape of this emotion. Just imagine it.

Once you have it, think about one of your flaws or defects. Think about it and see what appears; what do you see in your imagination? What comes to your mind? Still feeling the state of deep acceptance, look at this flaw with the emotion of acceptance. Transfer all of your acceptance to this flaw and feel that you consent to its existence. Feel the understanding that it is a part of you and you can come to like it. Accept this flaw fully. Once you're done, repeat this process to cover all of your perceived flaws the same way. You can repeat this exercise as many times as required.

Goal no. 2: Approve of yourself as you are at this particular point in life. No one else will truly accept you until you do.

Assertiveness

The next step, or perhaps a step simultaneous with the previous one, is self-expression. The better you know who you are, the more consciously you live and the more you accept yourself, the easier it will be for you to self-express. It also works the other way around—the more often you express yourself to others, the more consciously you will live and the more you can accept. One is connected with the other. Assertiveness is not a way to control other people, although it's often presented as such. It's a way of expressing yourself without attacking others. It's also the conclusion that you have equal rights as other people and the agreement to respect both your own and other people's rights. Self-expression can't be successful without a good discernment of your field of influence in relation to other people's and of where the border between yourself and other people is.

Start paying attention to how you show yourself that you are important to yourself.

In a situation in which you feel something's not quite right, ask yourself this control question: if I were truly important to myself, if I truly respected myself, would I act like that? If the answer is positive—alright. If it's negative, ask yourself how you could give more respect to yourself, your needs and your emotions. Here are some examples of situations in which you resign from being true or honest to yourself: you decide against saying something important to you at a meeting, even though you feel the need to, as you think that other people have more right to speak their minds than you. Or you agree to a meeting in a place inconvenient for you because your friends want to meet there, and you think if you proposed another spot, they wouldn't want to meet you, and so on.

What other people think of you doesn't usually matter. The only thing that matters is your idea about what's in their heads. Also, you will never know the truth. That's why you can build your self-esteem by changing the ideas you have about others and letting others spin their own ideas.

See how that works—the next time you are about to choose between your own convenience and other people's supposed thoughts and opinions, just imagine and assume that they are perceiving you positively. Find and write down a couple of thoughts that could positively describe what you are about to do. Don't limit your thoughts, and if a strange or exotic thought comes to your mind, note it as well.

Do what you feel like doing just as if it were certain that others would start admiring and appreciating you because of what you are about to do—and see what happens!

Additional TIP: **It might also be a good idea to schedule "no limit" days, time just for**

yourself, once in a while. Do everything that's "bad for you" or socially stigmatized; in other words, things your parents, friends or partner wouldn't accept. Things you love. It could be a two-hour bath or a Saturday spent in pajamas playing your favorite video games for hours... It will help you go back to your "disobedient childhood" and will symbolically free you from the social prohibitions that restrict you. Don't overdo it, though! ; -)

Goal no. 3: Don't hold yourself back from telling people about your needs, beliefs and ideas. Do what's in your best interest and don't look back. Know your boundaries and don't let anyone cross them. Don't be ashamed of what's innate in you.

Proactiveness

Focus on taking action. Here, again, we are discussing a situation in which one skill or mindset influences another one and they strengthen each other. If you are self-aware, if you know what you need and where you're headed, if you accept yourself even with all the things you don't like about yourself, then it will be much easier for you to take **real action** aimed at your goal. On the other hand, you will never discover certain things about yourself and about this world without real engagement in action. Taking action is the main foundation of both self-esteem and confidence in general; nothing can be changed without it! Every personal transformation or healing process is created through action.

Have the attitude, "I can do it, and if not, I will find a way to learn how to do it!"

It's about eyesight and mindsight. Eyesight is judging what you see, judging according to appearances. But mindsight is how you interpret what you see. And you can choose. It's all up to you.

As Henry Ford once famously said, "Whether you think you can, or you think you can't—you're right." Reinforcement of your self-belief requires two things: having the intention to believe in yourself, and takings actions to make this intention come true.

Take actions such as this exercise, for example: In order to free yourself from the limiting beliefs and opinions about your capabilities of your inner critic, write down what you desire the most, which, at the same time, appears to be something impossible to get. Then write down why it's impossible to get. Describe all the real obstacles you have encountered. Look at what you've written down and come up with at least three ways to move yourself towards this goal. Dare to see your influence and believe that you can do something. Take a step forward, even the smallest step! Will you dare to believe in yourself and make a change in this particular case that's so important to you? In the last chapter of this book you will find plenty of useful exercises. Some of them will require some of your time and effort. Will you be persistent and active enough to take the steering wheel of your own life and never let it go?

Goal no. 4: Focus on taking effective action regularly! Persistence and regularity are the key!

Responsibility

Many people resign from personal responsibility, thus trying to protect their self-esteem. This is their logic: "When someone else, not me, is responsible for difficult matters in my life, then I can keep thinking well about myself, or whining about myself and getting other people to cheer me up! There's someone else to be blamed and who's guilty; someone else destroys my life and my comfort! I don't have to do anything or change myself a bit, because it's all someone else's work! Ha! How convenient!"

At the first sight, it doesn't look like such a bad thing—I'm alright; it's someone else who is the "bad guy." **You have to realize it's a deadly trap though, because if "someone else is ruining my life," then that's the same person who has the power to repair it.** I can't do a thing; I play the role of victim and thus the feeling of self-esteem is inaccessible. Taking responsibility for your life comes down to looking at things through the prism of the questions, "What do **I** need?" and "What can **I** do to fix it?" Someone's ruining my life? OK, shit happens; now, how can **I** make it better? What can **I** do to overcome this situation?

Also, picking other people apart gives the impression of being a temporary fix for gaining self-confidence, but in reality it's a false confidence. This is your ego trying to sneak in and base your self-worth on the perceived lack of worth in others. So again, if you compare, you will never be happy.

At some point of my life, it dawned on me that my sole concentration needed to be on myself. I needed to put all of my energy into myself. You will, too; others are a distraction. You have spent long enough, as I had, putting energy into others in order to boost your self-esteem. Certainly, comparison is not always negative; sometimes you just look up to others to build your confidence in a positive way, which reinforces your own value as a contributing member of society. On the other hand, sometimes I just wanted to care of the people in my life. It is crucial for you to remember that you cannot take good care of others when you yourself are broken.

In order to strengthen your sense of responsibility for your life, you can write out significant things that make you mad, irritate or frustrate you, things you are not content with in your personal and professional life. Divide these situations into four groups:

-Situations you have control over and are trying to change.

-Situations you have no control over but are still trying to change.

-Situations you could have control over but that you don't do anything to change.

-Situations you have no control over and are not trying to change.

Now think, how often do you waste your energy on things you have no or very little control over? What's the outcome? What about the situations that irritate you that you could control but are not taking any reasonable action toward controlling?

What small steps could you take right now to fulfill some of your needs today? Make a bold decision to start taking action in the zone in which you have an impact, instead of throwing yourself into the sphere of "I don't have any control." Every single day when you experience frustration, ask yourself, "Can I change something that irritates me?" If you can, start taking action.

Responsibility helps you gain a positive attitude—an attitude full of acceptance, enthusiasm and good energy. When you experience a sense of discord about some action you are taking or are about to take, ask yourself this question: "Who made me do this? Who decided I would be doing this?"

The answer, contrary to appearances, will always be the same—**you** are making the choices. Even if your boss ordered or asked you to do something, it's you who finally made the decision (taking your own business into consideration first), "Yes, I will do it," or "No, I won't do it"—it's your call. Realizing this fact changes your perspective and attitude. Because if you are the one who chooses, why would you sabotage your own decisions? If you are feeling resistance, it could mean that you are about to do or are already doing something against your best interests. What does resistance tell you about your emotions and your needs? How can you fulfill them?

Here's another technique I use. It helps me free myself from the expectations I have of myself, other people and reality. And what's even more important, it helps me see how much I already have, and how much the things I have and experience in my life on a daily basis are great.

Whenever a bad thought appears in my head (e.g., "I'm not handsome enough") I ask myself what I would say about who I am right now 30 years from now. What would be my opinion of my "today me" as an older man? It makes me instantly notice how wonderful what I have now is. Or whenever I start to think about my limitations, about how I can't do this or that, I start thinking about someone who was in my life but is now gone, someone who can't experience even a bit of the life we live. Always take responsibility for your own perceptions and emotional states. It's always on you. Always look for a view that will help you gain more perspective and distance yourself from your problems.

Goal no. 5: Quit playing the role of victim and take ultimate responsibility for your life. That's the only way!

Coherence

Every one of us has a system of beliefs about what's important in life, what one should do, what's appropriate and what's improper. Theoretically, this system should determine our conduct and we should consider it all in our actions. In reality, though, that's often impossible and we often do things that are inconsistent with this system of beliefs. The more of these inconsistencies appear in your life, the more anxiety you feel and the more difficult it is to feel important and valuable. You can't build your self-esteem while ignoring **your own system of values**, doing things that you personally feel are wrong! For example, you may lack coherence if you're cheating on your partner and you feel that's wrong, or if you're constantly getting drunk or drugged up and doing things you think are detrimental, stupid, weak or downright pathetic.

"Am I mistaken in assessing what's happening to me now? Will I make the right decision?" Such doubts are all but uncommon in the life of a person who lacks self-trust. When you strengthen the pillar of coherence, you will start experiencing a peace coming from the deep belief that you know what's good for you better than anyone else. This of course doesn't rule out the possibility of gathering other people's opinions, feedback and points of view to help you form your own view. To develop self-trust, every time you are about to ask someone what you should do and how should you act, first ask the same question to yourself. And I mean really ask—aloud or in your thoughts, and wait for the answer. Dare to follow it; take responsibility for your decision and the choice that you have made. I truly believe the results will outgrow your expectations.

The last thing (and perhaps the most important!)—**STOP FAILING!**

How many times have you promised yourself you would change something, start doing sports, meet new people or travel more? How many times have you started losing weight and stopped after two weeks? How many times have you have set an alarm clock and then pressed "snooze" five times in a row, and arrived at the office late? How many times have you not kept your own word? How many times have you lied to yourself? How many times have you postponed all the things of the utmost importance to yourself—until next week, until next month, until next year, until never? You can't be coherent if you keep letting down the most important person in your life—YOU. How can you believe in yourself and trust yourself if you have been failing in every single extremely fucking simple aspect of your life for a couple of years now?

It doesn't work that way. Self-esteem comes from faith in your own words. If you decide to start running half an hour every day, you will become more and more confident with every passing day as you keep your promise. You will feel stronger and other people will also notice it. But when you quit, you will feel like shit. When you lie to other people and you cheat them or cheat on them, they remember.

So do you.

With every single resolution made and failed, it becomes harder and harder to trust yourself, and then, one day, you wake up as a grumpy, fat, frustrated balding man or an old witch, who destroys the joy of life by calling the police when someone throws a garden party three blocks away.

Goal no. 6: Realize what's important to YOU and strive to implement these values in daily activities! Keep all the promises you make to yourself. Make your own words MATTER to yourself!

Above you have six goals on which you can focus, depending on what's the most important to you at this moment in life. Work you do to improve one of these areas will pay off with an improvement in all the other areas, so where you start is not of the utmost importance. Even the smallest achievement on your way to any of these goals will improve your self-esteem.

Remember that **self-awareness**, understood as a recognition of your own resources, is crucial on this journey. You need recognition of and deep knowledge about your abilities and inabilities. Once you've got that, then there's time for self-acceptance. However, the stage of self-acceptance can be complicated. Because consider, you could arrange a plan of action divided into a certain number of steps, and thanks to your self-awareness you could estimate that, for instance, now you are on step number two. You could also come to the conclusion that what you originally thought was step three is really step two, because life has modified the original plan. Life sends you a piece of information: you're aiming too high; focus on what's possible. Now a new problem appears, because you can hear your mind whining, "You should've been on step number three already for a long time now!" And now yet another new fear arises, a fear that things are going too slowly. The words "should've" or "ought to" clearly state that you are dealing with a socially induced principle, imposed on you by other people. **Things, events and situations are not how they should be, they just are how they are.** If you can deal with that, then you can talk about real self-acceptance.

Mindfulness and awareness—the first two steps to real and healthy self-esteem

Let's dive even deeper into the true meaning of self-esteem.

Usually, people talk about manifestations of its absence.

Its absence is cited as the reason for all kinds of psychological problems—difficulties in relationships, anxiety, aggression, self-aggression, dependency, addiction, eating disorders, obsessive perfectionism, chronic dissatisfaction with life, and so on. But the explanation that the cause of our problems is usually lack of self-esteem doesn't give us any answer as to how to change it or how to overcome the problem.

The information that our self-esteem is formed mainly in childhood relationships with our parents doesn't help much either. It's valuable information for current parents of small children, but for grown-ups who want to build healthy self-esteem it isn't much help.

In every single family you can find, there was some flaw in the parents' behavior that contributed to a lack of, or a splinter in, a person's healthy self-esteem in their adult life. Sometimes these are real negligence or errors, but no matter how we evaluate them, there's nothing we can do to change what has already happened. Luckily, however, while it's true that self-esteem is formed during childhood in relationships with parents, it's also true that it continues to be built our entire lives and that as adults we become solely responsible for it.

So what should we do to build it?

As usual, when we ask for a solution—"What to do?," "How do I overcome or improve something?"—we must first precisely answer the question of the purpose of this "doing" or "improving."

An answer along the lines of "I will have better self-esteem" is too general to guide you on the way. What exactly does "healthy self-esteem" mean to you? What would have to change in your everyday life to clearly show you that now your self-esteem is much better and you have much more of it?

Let me help you a little bit in answering this question by showing you how you might understand healthy self-esteem. Unfortunately, I'm not the author of this graceful and accurate definition. It was formed by Nathaniel Branden (doctor of psychology, therapist, philosopher, and author of *The Psychology of Self-Esteem*).

He wrote:

"Self-esteem is the disposition to experience oneself as competent to cope with life's challenges and being worthy of happiness."

It's a great definition, as it allows us to clearly separate the meaning of self-esteem from the temporary and superficial feeling of complacency.

A person with low self-esteem will occasionally feel stronger, safer and more valuable. These feelings are usually the result of a given external circumstances, such as receiving praise or interest from someone, being successful in an endeavor, etc. However, these are short-lived feelings. Deep down this person feels like a crook. They feel they received something they don't deserve.

Whenever I look at the above definition of self-esteem, the first thing that strikes me is what should be the beginning of the self-esteem building process—experiencing oneself as a PERSON.

People with low self-esteem know surprisingly little about themselves. When talking to these people I often get the impression that they are much better attuned to the lives of the people around them than to their own.

These are usually the people who, when asked, "How are YOU?," answer, "My husband stopped drinking," "My kids just finished college," or "I can't take this anymore, because my wife wants ones thing, my daughter wants another and my son is a big mess." It's much easier for them to talk about what others want, think, go through and desire than about themselves.

Talking with these people, it's not rare to have the impression that they are "invisible," and that in relations with other people they don't exist as a real PERSON, who also has desires, plans, thoughts and emotions. It's like they don't know that they don't have to go along with what other people are going through all the time.

So, if you want to start building your self-esteem, start treating yourself as a PERSON—someone who lives with other people, someone who feels empathy, but is a separate being and has a life of their own. Start by getting to know and to FEEL yourself.

Start this fascinating process of feeling yourself in this very moment, by listening to your breath, by paying attention to the feelings that come from your body.

Finish reading this chapter, or give it a short break and sacrifice two minutes right now just to focus on accurately and carefully feeling yourself—just you and your body, in silence.

How's your body positioned? Do you feel comfortable? Which parts of your body are tensed? Also feel the parts of your body that touch the ground, the chair or the sofa and consciously feel the pressure you are exerting on what you're sitting, standing or lying on. Increase the pressure by sitting back—what change can you feel?

This mindfulness also helps the affirmations you've been saying finally start doing their job. Often, the reason they don't work comes from the above definition of self-esteem. Unless you can feel yourself as a person, unless you can feel your body and your present energy in the here and now, and it's your habit, your default state, you can't feel that you can cope with life and that you deserve all good things in the form of happiness, love, success and acceptance, because **those affirmations have no addressee.**

The sole practice of repeating, "I'm a great woman" or "I'm a fantastic man" won't make you believe it's true if you don't work on the foundations first. You won't be able to refer these affirmations to yourself, as you're lacking self-awareness, the linking point.

That's why I have homework for you. For the next couple of weeks do this exercise every day, becoming mindful and conscious of your breath, sensations and state, and realizing that you are a person, an entity separate from what surrounds you.

Physicality and self-esteem

Hormones affect your body **a lot**, no matter whether you're a man or a woman. The best effects in any personal change take place when regular mental work is combined with regular workouts and outdoor activities. This is called the holistic approach and it's been praised since forever, but we often tend to forget that some simple and cliché things really WORK. Everyone knows that "you should eat healthy and exercise," but hey, who really does that? We think we can outsmart nature, spending entire days sitting on our butts, eating crap food all the time and still feeling well. But we can't. People who don't exercise frequently lack the urgent motivation to do anything constructive. So often, they don't have any real deep problems with self-confidence or self-esteem and are neither disorganized nor lazy—it's just their hormonal fluctuation that sucks and leaves them without the motivation to take action. It's not that they were born shy or unable to do anything—it's about hormones. It's biological, all in your body's chemistry.

I often stumble across people who, after just one week of trying anything new, say, "I've been hitting the gym for a week now and I don't see any results," or, "I've gone running three times now and I don't feel any better!" It's a great excuse for not changing and a good rationalization for themselves and others in favor of surrendering and becoming a quitter. You don't always have to change things in your life, but if you really want to achieve something and adapt your system to regular sports and movement, you have to be persistent and keep exercising without quitting after just two months like a sulky little kid. It's elemental. It's crucial. It's as important as breathing. It has to be an integral part of your lifestyle, no excuses.

When you exercise regularly, your hormone levels normalize. You have more energy and more strength and in effect you attract much more success, new relationships and an overall feeling of confidence into your life. Your stress hormone levels are lowered and you feel much more relaxed, even though you might be physically more tired. Exercise is about starting from the basics, from the important sphere constituted by your body and its physical feelings and sensations.

No mentally sane person starts building a house from the second floor or from the roof. It only makes sense to start from the foundations. That concept is logical when you're thinking about a construction site, but not so easy to navigate when you're delving into the dark depths of your psyche.

Start communicating with your body and your breath—these two things connect you with the real world. Everything can be thought, even the craziest thing that comes to our mind; that's why the FEELING of physical sensations serves as a reality check. What does this mean for your self-esteem?

Real self-esteem **can only be built in contact with the feelings** of emotions and the body. Thoughts should cooperate with them. It's hard to start with thinking (e.g., affirmations), if you've lost touch with what's most fundamental.

So, as someone who just laid a foundation for a new home can't say, "I have built a house!," so you, just having started training your self-perception, can't say, "I have self-esteem!"

So train, exercise and don't stop—it will be a great anchor, allowing you to perceive yourself as a separate and independent human much more easily. And there's much more you can do in terms of movement and physicality.

Did you know that breathing itself can help you become much more confident in general?

Why? Deep breathing relaxes your tensed body and can't be resisted on a psychical level, assuming you breathe correctly. When you consciously take a deep breath, you are forced to focus on yourself and to distance yourself from the external world. The more consciously you breathe, the more control you have over your life. Literally.

Several times a day, take a short break to consciously catch a breath. Focus on the pelvis. Sitting or standing, with one hand at your back, at the top of your hips, breathe so the bottom of your belly rises (as if you were inflating a balloon). You have to feel the breath in your whole body, even the tips of your fingers. With every single breath, release your tension. Even three minutes of proper and deep breathing three times a day will relax you much better than a cup of coffee or a cigarette (in fact, those just stress you out even more). When breathing, learn to listen to your internal voice. Ask yourself, "How do I feel?" If the answer is "good," you will feel satisfaction coming from this statement. If you feel bad, ask yourself why and what you should do to change it.

When you focus attention on your body, observe your breath and start noticing all the places you feel the tension, tingling and itching. Then you might start feeling like moving your body a little bit.

Do it. Focus on the movement, on what it's like and where it's leading you, on how you feel afterwards, what changes occur and where exactly in your body they occur. Focus on how your breath changes. Don't try to force anything.

If you don't feel the need for any movements, don't try to force it; relax and wait. Give yourself some time. Maybe that's what you need right now. Or maybe you're feeling really comfortable right now. If that's the case, focus on the pleasure of the comfort you're feeling. During the course of any day, there are plenty of moments when your attention can be directed towards your body, your feelings and your sensations, and you can start building much greater self-awareness right away.

Examine your desire to move at different times during the day. While driving or waiting in traffic, at the bus stop, in a boring meeting, while waiting for your operating system to load up, on Sunday morning in bed... There are plenty of little moments, and plenty of different sensations (e.g., tingling, itching) you can use to focus on yourself (you don't have to close your eyes when you do it, although it might be helpful) and examine your need to make a small movement. This is a first step towards better self-esteem, but not the last.

If you have more time and enough space, you can experiment a little bit and make your movement bigger, wider, more extensive and more dynamic. See how it changes the way you feel and how you like it.

Some people may associate movement with coercion and pressure, as they've usually been forced to move (e.g., in school, or by their parents). But the truth is, movement is life and you need it. If you're an adult and you ignore it, it's frankly pathetic. So start noticing how you move. Ignore what other people say about the salutary influence of morning runs and just focus on your own movement, on the need to move that is inside you. Find it.

You can also take it a step further and do something more.

When you're focusing on your body and the sensations that come within, ask yourself what could be changed to make you feel more comfortable. What can you do in this very moment to make your body feel better? Do it. If you don't feel any better as a result, ask yourself again what could be changed. Always be looking for the best state. Take exactly what you need.

Seemingly, what you do in these first steps is only about your body, but that's not entirely true. By doing all these simple and banal exercises, you learn how to notice yourself, listen to your needs and take care of them proactively, on a daily basis.

You can learn much more about awareness of your body, along with other highly effective techniques I personally use on a daily basis, in my free 120 page e-book "Mindfulness Based Stress and Anxiety Management Tools." It's a foundation everyone should master for their own good, something that should definitely be taught to kids in public schools. After all, you can't run a marathon without shoes.

The social context

Let's think about the social context. In order to find a sense of security, you might feel the urge to assess your own value in relation to other people. Perhaps you're trying to get to know yourself through the prism of other people's lives. Maybe you observe their behaviors toward you and listen to words they say. You wonder what they can think about you and what you should do to make them think the best about you. **It's a dead-end road.** When you're led by the limiting belief that your worth lies in comparison to other people, the only things you will observe in yourself will be inferiority and low value. They are a source of low self-esteem.

Now, think about how you judge others. Write down your criteria of assessment. What makes people better or worse in your eyes?

So often we judge others just as we would judge ourselves. It comes down to criticizing in other people all the things we haven't accepted about ourselves. If, for example, a man doesn't accept his own sensitivity and other aspects of feminine energy, then these characteristics shown by other men will upset him.

Everything that bothers us about others is just an indication of our own unsolved problems. Carefully observe your own reactions in social interactions, and you will get to know yourself better. Self-knowledge is a very crucial thing in the process of building healthy self-esteem.

The assessment criteria

When we want to rate a movie we saw in a theater, we can do so in a number of different ways. We can rate the acting, plot, special effects, music, images and many other aspects of cinematography.

It shouldn't be much different when rating ourselves. We can self-assess using many different criteria. But what's interesting is that self-esteem is usually reduced to one, general feature: "I'm worthless," "I'm amazing and I rock," "I suck at everything." These generalizations are detrimental, as they make us blind to the whole big panorama of criteria that has to be taken into consideration to make our self-assessment accurate and meaningful.

Human beings very often identify themselves with a whole spectrum of values and material things, which are constantly being admired, cultivated and talked about in media and society. Everything is designed to make people feel worthless and insufficient—because only then do they become extremely susceptible to consumerism and drive the economy with their materialistic approach. They become much easier to control. You better escape this mindset as soon as possible.

Facts-based self-assessment

If you really want to rate yourself, stick to the facts. Don't tell yourself anything that isn't true. Healthy self-awareness and self-assessment can only take place when the relationship you build with yourself is based on a foundation of maximum honesty.

The belief that you're "not enough" only turns your attention to the evidence that confirms that. Every single belief works just like a pair of glasses, changing the optics of your perception. If you're looking for negative input, you will eventually find it.

For a change, try to find proof that you're enough, that everything's alright with you. But don't look for it in what other people think and say. Search for it in your own "backyard." Start with small things. The longer you ask yourself, "What proves that I am valuable?"

the more answers to that question you will eventually find.

<u>The development of healthy self-esteem should be carried out simultaneously on these two levels:</u>

- Getting to know your weaknesses, accepting them and treating them as an area of your life worth working on and developing to a level you are content with.
- Getting to know your strengths and learning how to fully appreciate each of them.

What's the best way to do those things? There are a few ways and all of them start with **awareness**. You have just learned more about the true meaning of healthy self-esteem and now you are able to observe your own thoughts, behaviors and reactions more consciously.

I encourage you to carefully observe your habits of thought every day.

Pay attention to how you think about yourself and other people. If this thinking doesn't serve you, then make improving your thought-patterns and beliefs the most important part of your self-development journey for the next few weeks or months.

The feeling of self-worth vs. self-esteem

In the English language the term self-worth is usually treated as a synonym of self-esteem.

In many other languages though (for example, in many Slavic languages such as Russian, Ukrainian, Belarusian, Polish or Bulgarian) the term "self-esteem" starts with the word "feeling" (literally "the feeling of one's dignity/value" – e.g. "чувство собственного достоинства" in Russian), which points to the sphere of experiencing and feeling emotions. The feeling of self-worth is **a state of mind, whereas self-esteem is an attitude towards oneself and an evaluation of oneself.**

Just as the feeling of anger can be a result of the thought, "He shouldn't have been so mean to me!," so the state of feeling one's self-worth comes directly from self-esteem (assessment of one's self-worth). As you can see, these terms are strongly interconnected with each other and on a more general level can be used as synonyms.

A milestone on the road to healthy self-esteem is the strong belief in your self-worth, which could be expressed, "I am worthy and I'm enough." If you have kids, make it a long-term goal to create this belief in your offspring's mind—it's one of the most important foundations of psychological health.

Unfortunately, when assessing our self-worth, we've been socially hardwired to base it on material possessions or external sources, such as income, cars, gadgets, certificates, number of friends, qualifications, degrees, social status, etc.

How many hours a day do you spend making yourself feel like a more valuable person? Most people spend their entire lives investing their energy in the Sisyphean task of building their feeling of self-worth based on external factors.

Shopping, language courses, certificates, gadgets, cars, careers... Can any of these things tell anything about your real value? Let's take a look.

Money doesn't make you a better man—it's amazing how our minds are susceptible to illusions, making us believe that pieces of paper or digital data make us better people than others. It's fascinating how numbers in bank account magically boost the self-esteem of their owners, who have often given away power over their own lives to money to achieve wealth. By no means am I stating that money is not important in our lives, but think about this: if you lose all of your life savings and properties, would that suddenly make you someone less valuable as a human being?

A new car doesn't make you more valuable—if someone stole your car, would that make you suddenly meaningless or less important as a human being? How could an item that doesn't really have anything to do with your interior and your personality contribute to your value? **If a rich dad buys his 18-year-old son a new Ferrari, does it make the son a better or a worse person? Neither; the car itself just doesn't matter. It's just a machine. Irrelevant.**

Jewelry and gadgets don't make you more valuable. What you own doesn't say anything about your inner value and potential. You can own the rarest and most beautiful jewels on this planet (maybe you inherited them?) and the most futuristic computers and phones out there—identifying yourself with their value is still an illusion and a big lie.

Having a huge amount of friends doesn't make you more valuable either… And the same goes for the quality of the relationships you have with them. Your friendships are an outcome of your habits—and depending on how open and social you are, you can have more or less of them. But does the fact that you have only one, really great friend instead of ten best friends make you a worse person? What if you feel that you really need to be alone for the next couple of months to write a book or record an album? And **can you measure the real inner value of men by counting all the people they know?** Think about all the geniuses of science and the arts who pushed the world forward or made it a better place with their great inventions, books, theories or music. They were often hardcore introverts who spent all their time in the comfort of their homes or labs.

Being promoted at work doesn't mean you are more valuable. It only means that maybe you will have different duties, maybe you will have more responsibilities and maybe you will be earning more pieces of paper or digital money. Other socially brainwashed people who still believe in the magical power of social status **might believe that you are someone else now**, but don't buy into that illusion—your worth hasn't changed a bit, apart from the fact that now you have a different, fancier label under your surname.

Knowledge doesn't make you more significant—you can close yourself up in a room for one year and read thousands of books. When you finally leave the room after that one year of reading, will you be a better person? Will your real value rise in any way? You can find any definition or rule in an Internet search in a matter of seconds. You can attain more knowledge at any moment and lose it at any moment. It doesn't really define your value.

Earning certificates and diplomas doesn't make you more valuable—the only thing the resulting papers demonstrating your knowledge prove is that you have spent a given amount of time and put a given amount of work into learning something new and passing the exams. Does that make you a better person, though? Is someone who chose a different form of education, or who never decided to acquire a degree, a worse person? Of course, gaining new knowledge is very important and can greatly improve your life—but applying for a course just to get a piece of paper and social approval doesn't have much to do with real self-development.

Looks? This is huge. Standards of beauty are constantly changing, messing with our heads and blowing our inborn self-esteem to smithereens. They constantly make us want to escape ourselves and be someone else. This is absurd. How can you be someone else? One hundred years ago chubby or even obese ladies were considered sex bombs. In the 2000s people looked with awe at anorexic models with their ribs and other bones visible. Nowadays, "fit" appears to be "the shit." Maybe in ten years enormous bodybuilding women with biceps bigger than their heads will be considered sexy. Or we will go back to standards from hundreds of years ago. Fifty years ago female tattoos were considered slutty, obnoxious and socially unacceptable. Today, people say they're cool and artistic. Man's fashion? Metrosexual? Lumbersexual? 50s gentleman? Muscular? Skinny and artistic? Outlaw badass? Tattoos? You name it. It constantly changes; you can't even follow all this madness. The point is—it never ends. Ladies fix their noses, just to find out two days later that their breasts are too small, their butts are too big, their legs are crooked, their hair looks bad, etc. You can never win this race, and it certainly won't lead to other people's acceptance. "It's impossible. It's pathetic. Like girls in stilettos trying to run."[2] Men? They open a magazine or watch TV and what do they see? Buy a new car, buy a new phone, and buy this expensive watch! And look, here's an image of a perfectly handsome and perfectly dressed man. He is leaving his expensive car and there are a whole bunch of insanely attractive girls waiting for him. He's a big deal, but what about you, ordinary Joe? Buy all these things and you will be, too! What

---

[2] Emily Haines & the Soft Skeleton – "The Lottery." A great song, by the way.

do these images do to your self-esteem? They shatter it.

The mere fact of you being alive is an extreme miracle and coincidence. You have legs. You have arms. You have eyes. Do you take those things for granted? There are wars around us, [hundreds of military conflicts taking place every day](). Realize how extremely lucky you are to be healthy and alive, walking on this planet. It's all about attitude.

I have two friends, seemingly very similar—both short, balding, ginger redheads. From the common social point of view—ouch! But they represent two opposite attitudes. One of them is constantly depressed. He feels bad; he feels he lost his life the day he was born. Because of his negative attitude, he attracts even more bad situations and, of course, blames everything on his looks. The other guy, however, made this trait his unique attribute. He often tells beautiful ladies how lucky they are to have met him, because he's so special. All the other men are black-, brown- or blonde- haired, or bald. But he's ginger. He's different; he's unique. He also tells them that it's said that ginger redheads are the best in bed... and every time I see him say this, it works. He's rarely alone when he doesn't want to be. He made a personal advantage out of something he once used to hate about himself, something he couldn't really change.

And all the things you can change, you have to accept first anyway. If you don't—you will keep beating yourself up and you will be much more likely to fail. Moreover—tell me who invented and where they wrote down such things as "perfect male and female measurements"? Is there any holy book or a constitution that says what "perfect man" and "perfect woman" mean? No. It's all temporary bullshit and it's all business. Who makes big money on this? Businesses. Society screws you. It's all about money—their money. Hence, don't be surprised that you don't get to read or hear such opinions about self-esteem as the ones in this book too often. They are simply not in the interest of anybody's profit. Undervalued people spend incomparably more money. **That's why it's not easy to persist in these beliefs, as nothing is on your side!** You simply open a newspaper, see an ad and there it begins.

The key is to look at yourself in the mirror and say, "You know what? I really like you. No, damn it, I love you, my friend! If we want to change, we can do it, but I already love you!"

Even all the things listed above (money, looks, cars, friends, etc.) brought together won't

increase your worth. I know, it might sound really terrifying for your good ole' value system. **But do you really want to follow systems that will lead you nowhere?**

QUIT value systems according to which without external boosters you are a worthless person, according to which you should have sacrificed your life to gathering knowledge, money and social contacts **ONLY to appear superior in other people's eyes, only to feel better just because of that superficial "social acceptance."** There's a psychological reason it can't work—you are creating an idealized image of yourself (e.g., yourself with a perfect, godlike body) and it brings you down, because you're constantly comparing yourself to this idealized, perfect image. It covers the diamond that's inside you with an old, stinky rug and tells you that you should be someone else. But ironically, to become somebody else (in the positive meaning of being the best version of yourself, not someone "perfect"), you have to first feel and accept the reality.

When you see a newborn baby, the category of this human being's so called "worth" or "value" dissolves— you can't define whether this baby is valuable or not, because it's unconditionally valuable; it can't be more or less worthy of something.

You don't have to believe that anything external gives you any lasting value, because that's when you forget about the real value you already have.

Of course, to quit boosting your self-esteem with external factors might seem like something close to impossible to you, but with time you will start noticing the value in yourself. At the same time, you will gradually stop finding it in material possessions, certifications, jobs or numbers of Facebook friends. You can barely imagine how liberated you will feel.

Hence, the most important step in finding your own self-worth is to finally understand that your value is and has always been there, inside you—more precious than anything else, untouched.

You are, have always been and will always be worthy—unconditionally. You are a human being who got a chance to live on Earth. Make that enough of a reason to appreciate your unlimited value. Close your eyes and check out how great you feel when you say to yourself, **"I'm unconditionally worthy." Say it every day.** Welcome to the world where the feeling of self-esteem is something natural and real.

Only then, when you feel that unconditional appreciation of yourself and your life, can you really start the journey of self-actualization. Make money, improve the way you look, meet new people, gain knowledge, and so on—but then, you will be doing this **truly for yourself, not for other people,** not just to start feeling good about yourself, just for a moment. You will stop caring about getting the reward **candy** for a trick, and will instead fully welcome the **grace** that's always been inside of you.

It's only then that you truly understand that all these external factors were never giving you the feeling of confidence—**you were the one giving it to yourself from the very start**, every single second! You were the one responsible for receiving the sense of confidence, no one and nothing else! You may have thought you felt confidence when certain external factors were present; you allowed yourself to feel it then, because your socially conditioned mind thought those factors were so important to society, and was inhibiting the emotion of confidence until you felt their presence, making you another cog in the machine that drives society forward.

<u>Moreover, when you finally understand this, all of your thoughts, actions and feelings will originate from</u>

<u>the mindset of abundance, not scarcity. And that's the "sweet spot."</u>

You will be doing these things **just for sake of doing them**, just to improve your life, just to play the game, just to feel even better than you normally feel, to feel even more excited and joyful; but if you lose the game, when you fail at something, or when things go differently than you expected—you will still be fine, peaceful, feeling good with yourself, grateful and present. The emotional fluctuation, the anxiety, and the feelings of dependency and uncertainty will be gone.

The extraordinary relation between self-acceptance and stress

Self-acceptance means being at peace with yourself, apart from the facts of who we are and who we want to be. It's the lack of unreasonable and overly high expectations of yourself. It's focusing on yourself and appreciating yourself for who you already are, instead of focusing on idealistic version of yourself.

Self-acceptance comes from being caring and forgiving towards yourself. To be forgiving and caring, you have to first deeply understand yourself.

You need to know the motives of your actions and the backgrounds of your reactions and behaviors, your thoughts and emotions. If you don't understand why, for example, you are bored when you start practicing your piano skills, you could judge yourself negatively—"It's probably because I'm just a lazy butt!"

When you know yourself well enough to come to the realization that piano isn't one of the things that makes your heart beat faster, you are more forgiving—you don't judge and don't bring yourself down for "being a quitter." That's why self-observation, which leads to self-understanding, is an absolutely necessarily basis for healthy self-acceptance.

The lack of self-acceptance, and the resulting continuous, excessive demands and self-criticism, always work as a brake on your true potential. Only through understanding your own actions will you learn to accept your (sometimes bad) decisions and behaviors.

Do you sometimes get pissed off at someone because of their irritating behaviors or poor decisions? I bet you do! Take a moment to think about why you get so angry at these people. I guess you're probably thinking, "He/she shouldn't have done that!"

Take a moment to think about times when you don't accept other people's behaviors.

It's usually when you don't understand or accept their actions and the reasons behind them. You don't know what are they guided by and their actions seem pointless to you. Taking your knowledge about a given situation into account, you are convinced that the person should act differently. But it isn't always the case.

Now, try to remember a situation in which, at the beginning, you couldn't accept someone's behavior or decision, but after having a conversation with them, your feelings changed completely. How did it happen?

Most likely that person explained the motives of their actions to you and told you about the thoughts and feelings they had when making the decision that upset you. They showed you elements of the jigsaw puzzle you were totally unaware of.

You then understood, and in result—accepted them. Understanding leads to forgiveness, and thus, to acceptance. That's exactly how self-acceptance works.

When you don't know yourself well enough, it's hard for you to accept your own actions if they don't bring about the desired results. If you don't understand why you ran out of motivation again, why strong emotions took control of you again, why it's difficult for you to make new friends—it will be easy to criticize yourself for these failures. It will be natural for you to build up remorse and self-criticism.

That's why the art of self-acceptance largely comes down to getting to know yourself and learning about yourself. It's the art of self-inquiry. To be tolerant of yourself, you have to understand why you think, feel, act and behave in one way and not another.

Do you know what's interesting and strange and the same time? **The vast majority of people have no idea who they are and how they are!** What they REALLY desire, what sits inside their heads—they are unaware of these things! What they know, though, is how they SHOULD be. And that's what they focus on. It's truly a great recipe for low self-esteem!

The key here is insight into your own thoughts and feelings. I encourage you once again to take the challenge of understanding your own emotions, decisions and behaviors. A much better relationship with yourself is the main prize here! You need to see yourself in the right perspective and accept what you see.

People are equally afraid to recognize both their weaknesses and their strengths. They feel uncomfortable speaking about their strong sides and they are afraid to fall into overconfidence. They lessen their achievements and quickly find counterarguments for every single compliment they get.

At the same time, they feel the urge not to notice what remains after rejecting their positive and strong sides. They work out a number of ways to stop feeling themselves—they use stimulants and other chemical substances, overeat, drink, smoke, focus on other people and their thoughts, needs and expectations; they tense their muscles and are either constantly on the run, or languishing in front of a screen and living in an imaginary world. These are ways to remain in the sphere of not experiencing, effectively lowering your self-esteem, generating anxiety and helplessness.

So if you want to feel better, welcome everything that comes to you and don't resist it. Stop trying to explain why something happened and why it happened to you; don't fight it. Take the attitude of an observer and allow the feelings and images to flow freely.

When you feel angry, ashamed, or afraid, stop running away from these emotions. Focus on them! How do you feel each of these emotions, where is it in your body, what happens to you when you experience it? How do you know that you are angry, ashamed or afraid? Observe all that comes to you, just like you would observe clouds in the sky. [Learn how to do it and make it your daily habit!](#)

The enormous importance of self-support

The simplest things are often underestimated by the mind, as it doesn't believe they're worthwhile or they could work at all.

One of the issues I usually notice while working with people is that in the moments when things are going badly, when something's not right—no matter where the fault lies—these are the moments when real support and love are the most needed, **when your own support and love** are the most needed. Unfortunately, these are usually the moments when we give ourselves the least support and love!

When a good friend or a close family member comes to us with a problem we might as well have ourselves, we always find at least a few moments to hug that person, tell them how much we love them, how they can count on us and that they will surely overcome their problems. Interestingly, when the same happens to us, for some reason we get an amnesia attack. For some reason, we wring our hands and tell ourselves that we don't know what to do. These are the moments when we don't know how to support ourselves, how to express affection, how to tell ourselves an encouraging word. Instead of love, support, acceptance and warmth we give ourselves negation, lots of bad emotions and negativity— **exactly when we need to feel our own support the most!**

You are the only one who can truly help yourself. You are the one you are waiting for. Even if you receive help or advice from the outside, if the things you hear or read resonate with you, still you are the only person in the world who can apply all that wisdom to your life. You are the one who can take the light, keep it lit and carry it through your life, so it becomes your everyday habit!

In all these moments when things are falling apart, when things don't go your way—don't turn your back on yourself! Next time something bad happens, do something new, something you are not used to doing—**give yourself understanding, give yourself forgiveness, give yourself relief, and just give yourself love.** So often the things we do to ourselves in difficult situations are things we wouldn't do to our worst enemy! The things we tell ourselves, the way we treat ourselves when we start losing control—these are often things we would never say aloud even to people we hate. So how can you feel good in difficult moments, when the most important person in your life, the person that can help you the most, slaps you down, admonishes and kicks you from all sides?

How different would be your day if you woke up half an hour earlier just to spend it with yourself? People say, "I don't have time!" You have time. If you have time to scroll down Facebook, write text messages or watch TV for hours, then you certainly have 20 minutes for yourself. How different would be your day if you woke up early in the morning and gave your body a glass of water with freshly squeezed lemon juice? How different would your day be if you, when shaving or doing your make-up, looked at yourself with admiration, just as if looking at yourself for the very first time in your life? How different would your day be if you, while doing this, sang your favorite song and danced like nobody's watching? If you took a walk in the morning, stopped for a while, looked at the sky, listened to the birds and the wind in the trees?

Find five things you are grateful for every single day, things you already have in your life! It will alter your perception, and let you see all the things you already have, instead of looking at your life as something broken to repair. Always be looking for new miracles to discover. Your mind will have a problem with that, but remember that there are always hundreds of things to be grateful for! Hundreds of things you take for granted and don't even notice. Train your mind to focus on these things—it's a skill just like everything else.

I recently heard a blurb on the radio that said, "Grateful people are more satisfied in life and report being generally happier than less-grateful people." It gave me an idea, and one that has actually truly contributed towards my daily outlook on life: I began my own personal "thankfulness jar." I cut lined 3x5 index cards in half, and every day I would date them and write something I was grateful for THAT DAY. A rule I gave myself was that it could not be too generic, such as "I am grateful for my health," or "I am grateful for the pretty sky." I had to find a specific thing from that exact day to be grateful for so I could put the card in my jar. And do you know what? I began to see things as moments to be grateful for, whereas prior to that those moments simply felt like the everyday interactions of life.

For example, I remember shopping at one of those buy-in-bulk warehouses near the end of the day; it was a crowded and busy day since a holiday was coming up shortly. I bought several smaller items and at checkout, the nice lady asked me, "Would you like a box for your things?" and I simply, pleasantly, and normally replied, "Yes, please." She got a slightly surprised look on her face, which I did not really understand, then a moment later she said to the cashier and to me, "Do you know what? I've been working an eight-hour shift all day, and I do believe that yours is the first 'yes, please' I have received all day!" I was aghast—this poor, kind, hardworking girl was pleasantly serving people by doing her job at the very end of the retail day in a very busy shopping season, and yet somehow I was the first person to give her a simple "yes, please"? I made sure to re-affirm my appreciation for the compliment and to thank the staff again, and then I went on my way home. But I will tell you what—I had a wonderful encounter to write down for my thankfulness jar that day!

Seek out moments to be grateful for, and they will come to you. This consistency of actions will be a force within your life that begins to build bridges in places you did not even know existed. Life's an ocean, sometimes calm and sometimes stormy, and maybe your boss is a jerk and you would like to punch him right in the face, but your perception of all these things will be totally different if you build a healthy relationship with yourself—if only you start your day with meeting yourself and do everything to become your own best friend; if only you start going everywhere with the person who loves you, accepts you and always supports you. Because you are the person you spend every single moment with, you are the person you dance your entire life with!

I once purchased a simple little candle that had an affirmation written on it; the author of the affirmation is not known. However, during times of trial, this has personally helped every single person I have shared it with, and so I will also gift it to you, wishing you peace if you ever need to use it for yourself:

"This burden on my heart is too heavy to hold. I allow my spirit to grieve the loss of this dream. I allow my tears to cleanse me, freeing me from these crippling emotions. I release my expectations of the future and embrace the gifts this challenge has given me."

I think it's powerful. Take it away with you.

How to protect your self-esteem when life brings you down

When life grinds us into the ground with tons of problems, we usually expect our close ones to support us and cheer us up. That, among other reasons, is why we form relationships—to support each other.

Unfortunately, it doesn't always work as we'd like it to and sometimes our partner seems to be doing something opposite to what we'd like and what they (seemingly) should do. That's when we have to deal not only with our own issues, but also with the reactions of the people we love and respect.

For example, say Ann has been troubled by unemployment for a long time now. In consequence, her relationship has started to crumble. She feels like she does everything she can, but still she often hears that she's not ambitious enough for her partner and that her attitude is pathetic. She doesn't know if this is supposed to be a way to motivate her (that might be her partner's opinion), but her emotions are depressed.

Ann's self-esteem is now subject to a big trial—it gets lowered by her long unemployment from one side, and by the comments of her partner from another. The lower it initially was, the harder it will now be to deal with such a difficult situation—a situation in which healthy self-esteem is crucial, as it decides if Ann will be able to find a job soon. What should she do in this situation?

It would be a good idea to carefully observe how these comments affect her, and focus on what happens to her energy during these conversations—does she feel more or less energetic as a result? The fact that the comments are mean doesn't mean they're bad. A comment that awakens our anger can be indeed a great source of motivation, **but** not always and not for everyone.

If her husband says that it's his effort to motivate her, then maybe he's one of these people motivated by criticism and negative feedback. By the way, maybe Ann should take this into consideration and use it in situations when she supports her man, and slightly criticize his actions or behaviors instead of caressing him like a little kid.

What works for her husband doesn't have to work for Ann as well. For her, strong criticism might work as a de-motivator. She can notice it by focusing on her energy level and her will to take action—if they slope downward when she is criticized, she should start defending herself. This can be done in a few different ways, and she can choose the ones that seem to be applicable in a certain situation.

Don't listen to evaluations; ask for information

If someone says, "You are not ambitious enough" or "Your attitude is pathetic," then they haven't really told you anything at all. These evaluations are so general that they can't be practically used for anything or applied in any way, apart from taking them as a bullet to the knee and repeating in your mind how "unambitious" and "pathetic" you are.

Your goal is to protect your self-esteem in this situation, so you can't allow yourself to repeat these words in your internal dialogues. So anytime you listen to general statements like these, you need to ask the person who throws them at you to tell you what exactly they have in mind and what should be done in this situation, according to them.

In this case Ann could ask her husband:

- "So what should I do according to you?"

- "What exactly do you want to convey by saying this; when exactly do you think I was not ambitious?

- "What does it mean that my attitude is pathetic? Exactly which situations do you have in mind?"

Usually these questions make the criticizing person think deeply about what they really want to say, and either they give more constructive feedback or withdraw from what they said earlier.

So often people throw their opinions around without even giving them a thought, sometimes using them more to discharge their own emotions than to build a dialogue with another person. By starting a discussion in such situations, you teach the other party to be more mindful and you protect yourself from this kind of unconstructive and pointless criticism both in this very moment and also in the future.

Ask about the purpose of the criticism

In the given example, "You are not ambitious enough," these words don't necessarily have to convey any criticism at all—they are only painful when the person who hears these words appreciates ambition as such and craves to be perceived as a "very ambitious person." It's a good moment to stop for a moment and think to what extent the pain is well-founded, and to what extent it's the effect of an oversensitivity of a kind.

However, the words "you are pathetic" are aggressive. When someone crosses our boundaries with their aggression, especially in face-to-face situations, it's very important to point that out and defend yourself.

These attacks are not always caused by bad intentions; sometimes people get carried away by a wave of their own emotions and hurt their loved ones simply because of that. So it's a good idea to start defending yourself by forming simple questions or statements about our feelings and emotions:

- "Why are you talking to me that way?"

- "What do you want to achieve by relating to me so aggressively?"

- "Do you intend to offend me?"

- "I really feel hurt when you talk to me that way and I don't feel like continuing this conversation, if you want to keep it so aggressive."

Let's say Ann asked her husband these questions and got an answer along the lines of, "I want to motivate you so that you can finally get a job and we can kill the tension that's been rising between us." The rest of this conversation should be focused on how Ann perceives this kind of motivation, what really motivates her and what her husband could do to really show her support and help her in this difficult situation.

Quit what doesn't work

Sometimes it also happens, both in intimate and casual relationships, that a person we need support from is simply not capable of giving it to us, usually in situations where our problem triggers strong emotion in that person and they just can't control themselves.

It's possible that Ann's long unemployment has become a serious problem for her husband. He might feel that he's the one person supporting and feeding the whole family, and thus he might be afraid that at some point he could fail, or that he could also lose his job for one reason or another, and that's when the real trouble would start.

It's also possible that he used to build his own self-esteem on Ann's resourcefulness: "My wife is so strong and smart; she's so unique!," or he perceived her as much more attractive when she was less available because she was busy with her work and she wasn't always at home waiting for him. We can't know for sure, and it's hard to definitely determine what might be the personal issues of the husband of an unemployed wife who used to earn a good salary before she got fired. However, when this kind of problem comes along, it can be a source of many strong emotions and expectations, which in turn will make focusing on his wife's needs much more complicated and difficult. So it's possible that every conversation about Ann's problem will trigger negative comments from her husband, **not because he doesn't respect her, but because he's taking her problems too personally.**

When talking about a problem triggers aggression in a person close to us, it can be a sign that maybe that's not a topic to be talked about with that particular person. Contrary to popular opinion, **we can't**

always talk about everything with our significant others! It's natural and it's OK if only we accept that.

When someone doesn't have the inner strength to deal with the emotions a given problem causes, it's also not too wise to expect they will be successful in supporting you. And it doesn't mean you can't continue being together and building a great relationship.

How to stop taking things personally

If you are tired of constantly thinking about how others will react to what you do, or feel that you constantly have to defend yourself from people's criticism, you probably take things personally. You treat everything others do or say too seriously.
Notice how the situation changes when you shift your attention from yourself to the other person. For instance, people often get mad when someone says "no" to them and they face a refusal.
When someone says, "I don't have time for you right now," it can be understood as an update about this person's situation—they don't have time and that's it.

It doesn't have to be anywhere close to the meaning you might decide to give it, for example, that you are not important to that person. This "importance" is something that you simply added to the original message, something that entered your brain neither through your ears nor your eyes. It was already there in your mind. It's simply a bad interpretation of what you've heard. The truth is that interpretation happened quickly and automatically, without you even giving it a thought, and it's also true that you might even think the person actually said that.

Always listen carefully! There's **nothing about anyone being or not being important** in "I don't have time for you right now"!

You're saying that it has the same meaning to you? Maybe to you, but does it mean the same for the person who said it? You don't know that. If you think you can read minds, then contact the James Randi foundation, prove your abilities and collect one million euros. Then you can give me a call and say, "Thank you for this easy money, man!"

Instead of playing a clairvoyant—you can **ask**. If you do this **calmly, without attacking the person or implying anything**, then you can find out what "I don't have time for you" **really** means.

Think about what you **add** to what other people say. How long now have you been doing that? What happened before and with whom that makes you so ready to start feeling rejected?

Does the situation that fuels your doubts concern what is happening right now, in relation to the person who said something that upset you, or does it concern something different? Something that happened in the past? Really think about it.

We often fear rejection when we feel doubtful about our own value or importance. Something that arises only in your own head is often projected onto your significant others. As a result, you really start feeling that's what they think. **But you don't know other people's thoughts.** All the assessments and judgments of yours that were never said aloud by anyone are only your own opinions about yourself.

How to deal with jealousy

Jealousy may concern a relationship, but it can also be concentrated on other people, sometimes strangers, who might have something precious to us. When you feel envy towards someone, it becomes very difficult to build or maintain a healthy relationship not only with that person... but also with yourself. Jealousy induces hostility and oftentimes accusations or sulkiness caused by the fact that someone already has something that we need or desire.

These accusations don't even have an addressee—because who's guilty of the fact that you don't have something? The person who has it? "Fate"? Yourself? Maybe each of these people and factors, a little? Jealousy leads us to cursing others, the mythical "fate" and ourselves. It's neither too constructive nor too smart, as it takes our power away and makes us feel like victims.

What to do?

The easiest solution would be "not to be jealous."

You can find a lot of "great advice" like that in popular magazines, outsourced blogs or bad self-development books. Q: "How to live happily?" A: "Don't be jealous!" The problem is you usually can't stop feeling what you feel, just like that. Attempts at silencing and suppressing our emotions by brute force, without any insight, usually end up badly.

If you often feel envious, realize that's jealousy and think about what exactly makes you feel it. For example, if you're a woman, let's say that you might feel bad because your beautiful friend just got pregnant and you're still single and not getting any younger. If the beauty of your friend is a trigger, you should get deeper into this feeling and ask yourself what's beneath the notion, "She's so beautiful."

She's beautiful and pregnant—what does this mean to you? What kind of thoughts and fantasies does it trigger in you when you think about these aspects of her life?

When you look at other people, you only see a tiny section of their lives. You don't start being jealous because they have something, but because YOU DON'T. Interaction with someone who already has "the thing" brings to life this desire and regret coming from the fact that this need is not yet satisfied. Envy pushes us towards fantasizing about the people who have what we want and often towards imagining that we live their lives.

So you are dealing with your needs and your fantasies—the very person you tend to think about is only a trigger that makes these thoughts appear in your mind. You are not jealous of their lives; you only mourn over the fact that you don't have what you just imagined. So you could just as easily go from feeling jealous to minding your own business and your own needs, from concentrating on others to focusing on yourself.

When you shift your attention from someone else to yourself, your ambitions and fantasies, you take the first step to dealing with your jealousy and other toxic feelings—because only your life and your feelings are things you can have control of.

When your attention is on somebody else's life, you can't do anything. When you focus on your friends having certain things that make them happy, you can only howl at the moon with grief, because the sphere of other people's lives isn't yours and you can't act there.

You can also put this energy into destroying someone else's happiness, but it won't result in you feeling any better permanently, maybe just for a few days, only before you notice that other people also have something that you could be jealous of... There are people who fill their lives with destroying everyone around them, but it doesn't solve anything in their lives, just makes them more and more miserable. The sooner you focus on yourself, the better.

Awareness and self-focus

This entire practice of "self-focus" is not a pleasant thing at the beginning. **Your attention escapes to**

external things simply because facing yourself can be difficult. That's what people do. They ESCAPE from their own problems on a daily basis, and that makes their lives miserable. People often prefer to ignore all of their flaws and choose eternal self-deception over facing the truth like adults do, and finally being able to start repairing their lives. During first the moments of the process, you have to feel your frustration and all your unsatisfied needs, but this awareness will allow you to break your chains and move on further, beyond that.

It's not about immersing yourself in your pain, diving into the thought that life denied you this or that and constantly thinking how badly you want it. It's about coming to the realization of what it is that you REALLY want and coming to the conclusion of what to do with all this "wanting." You have to think deeply about whether it is something you can achieve, or something you have no control over.

There are some deficits in our lives we have control over, and some we don't. There's ALWAYS some area of frustration in everybody's life. If you want to live peacefully, you need to learn how to live with it.

For example, someone lonely can suffer because of the emptiness and everyday silence in their home, while a family guy can suffer from lack of his own private space and free time.

Someone who doesn't have a car has to deal with city transportation, while someone with the car has to deal with traffic jams, regular repairs and the costs of maintaining the vehicle. There's NO PLACE IN LIFE where ALL of your desires can be fulfilled; there's always some kind of frustration, and happiness is about giving more attention to what we have and what we control than to what we don't have and are powerless against.

Change or acceptance? Make your choice

So when you come to the conclusion that you're missing or lacking something, think about whether you are going to accept it or to change it.

Acceptance of the deficit is about changing the areas of life you have control of and accepting the things you can't change. For example, if the condition of my wallet doesn't allow me to shop in certain exclusive stores and I know that what they sell won't be available to me for at least the next several years, I don't even look in their shop windows. Instead I go to the shops I can afford to shop at. I could never understand a friend of mine who sometimes spends hours tormenting himself with the prices in one of the exclusive brand shops, where wrist watches cost about $8,000 and more. I think he should just stop going there or anywhere near there, at least until he can easily afford anything from there without killing his financial solvency. What's the point?

On the other hand, if you come to the conclusion that you have some control over one of your deficits, even the faintest one, and deep inside you feel like you should satisfy this need, make this your goal and start going towards getting it, deliberately and decidedly.

The person you envy can become your source of inspiration in how to get there. Instead of fantasizing about how happy that person is with what they have (because they surely also have their area of dissatisfaction), always be looking for information about how they got it, and see what can you learn from their experience.

Regarding the example given above, if your friend is "beautiful," think about what she does to achieve her beauty. Does she regularly attend yoga classes and do CrossFit every two days, with no excuses? What's her diet? Maybe she doesn't eat crappy processed food and watch TV all day? There's always a PROCESS behind the EVENTS we see. We see musicians earning millions during big concert tours in just a few months, but we don't see the thousands and thousands of hours they spent practicing their instruments when their friends were drinking and partying; we don't see long days of rehearsals, hundreds of hours in recording studios, all the countless rejections they had to face, and so on. If your friend has a great partner or husband, what did she do to find him? Maybe they met in a library, not in a nightclub? Maybe he's not that great at all, they are not really happy together and she's just pretending? You would be surprised to know how little people are willing to speak about their unhappiness to others and how badly they want to maintain their image of having a "perfect life." Anyway, ask yourself this question: of all the things she does or did, what can YOU do?

Also look for other sources of knowledge and how-to. Take the examples of other people as well, not just this one person. You can fulfill many of your needs and desires, you can have many things of all the things other people have, but it requires your action and your patience. You can have almost everything in this life... but not everything all at once!

Jealousy usually happens "here and now"—"I want this **now**!" The question is whether you want to fight for it, go out of your comfort zone and start turning your dreams into precise goals for yourself. There's always a price to pay for each dream and the "behind the curtain" scenes you don't get to see at first.

Sometimes there's nothing bad in staying inside of your comfort zone—but it has to be done deliberately and your thoughts have to be guarded. If you feel the sting of envy despite your decision, think about what made you decide against going for it.

Moments when you consciously notice the feeling of envy can be a good motivation to take action and change your previous decision to stay in your comfort zone.

Stop pretending and begging for acceptance!

She's young, attractive and ambitious, but doesn't believe in her own value. When she has to ask someone for help, she imagines aggressive reactions and doesn't believe that someone will treat her with friendliness. She believes she can't start appreciating herself before she gets as independent and self-reliant as she wants to be.

While not asking questions and not asking people any favors, not only does she feel anxious and lonely, but she also gets left behind. She looks enviously at her colleagues when they ask other people for help without any hesitation and take what they want freely. She can't break the ice. Every time she asks about something or asks someone a favor, she feels weakness and inferiority. She expects that other people will take advantage of their position to neglect her, shout at her or reproach her that she's interrupting and should take care of her own business. It's easy to understand that she doesn't want to take the risk.

Can she stop worrying and caring about what other people think and do, and start taking care of her own business much more effectively? Of course she can; such a change is entirely possible. She only has to stop pretending, because that's where the trouble starts. She has to approve of herself, being as she is.

She says:

"I pretended to be so independent and self-sufficient, but that's not really the case…"

If you're not so independent and self-sufficient, then what and how are you actually?

And she replies, "I'm worthless," or something along those lines. This is just as untrue as the statement that she's entirely independent and self-sufficient.

If you have problems with self-esteem, then you certainly swing between unreal and biased visions of yourself. Usually this swing is driven by external things. When you are experiencing acceptance, you hear praise and see smiles and welcoming gestures; when someone hugs you or congratulates you, while patting you on the back, you burst with pride and you can already see brightness in the future. You feel some kind of inner peace and you smile often. This is a very good feeling, but it won't last much longer than the pat on the back you received. You know well that you have to work hard for other people's acceptance, and that you can't spend too long appreciating the moment of acceptance, because you have to run for the next one... and then another.

What happens when instead of words of praise, you just hear a grumpy murmur, and you see someone making a mean face? You will instantly fall into a deep despair—"I'm no good for anything!"—or you start being angry with yourself—"How could I do such a thing? I'm so dumb!"

In this way the reactions of other people become extraordinarily important to you, because they affect how you feel and your self-image. You cannot be indifferent to other people's whims or their smallest gestures. Your ears are well-trained to hear tones of acceptance and rejection in other people's voices. You can see all the tiniest movements of somebody else's face, and your mind never stops responding to the question, "What do these reactions say about me?"

You have some ideas about what people react to in a positive way and you are trying to create your image to please them, to make them react so more often. It can be an image titled "independent person," "smart person," "energetic person," etc. You are afraid to go beyond such a scheme, because you don't know what the reaction might be, and their reaction is very important to your peace of mind.

Asking questions and favors is a situation in which you expose yourself to other people's mercy and show them that they might have something you don't. This is the situation of opening and unveiling your "weak spot," and because you have a tendency to think about yourself in extreme ways, you feel like you are all this "weak spot" and there's no strength in you.

You will feel your power only when you get someone else's approval, but what if the reaction is not what you expected and that person is mean to you? Quite risky, isn't it?

What can you do?

You need to create your own strong self-image, so it doesn't get wrecked by other people's reactions. Those reactions can obviously be very different, sometimes friendly and sometimes hostile, and they will often depend on external things that you have no control of. When a person makes a mean face when you ask about something, it doesn't have to mean a lack of acceptance or approval. That person might just have a terrible stomachache or might have been upset by someone else beforehand. It would be quite stupid to think badly of yourself just because someone has diarrhea or has argued with his wife earlier that day. How can you build a strong self-image? Let's start with pretending—who do you pretend to be, apart from being aware that you are not that? Let's say that, for instance, you are not so "strong, self-sufficient and independent" as you'd like to be and as you would like others to perceive you to be.

Now, stop treating this feature as something binary (that's either 0 or 1, either black or white, either perfectly good or totally wrong, etc.), and treat it instead as something gradable. You are not totally strong, not totally weak, but more or less strong on many different levels, depending on many things.

There are many levels of strength and independence, and maybe you don't have it all at the level you'd like it to be, but still you are on some other level, somewhere in between.

Think about your strength

Think about all those situations when you've had to face adversities, when you've had to mobilize and get your crap together, when you did something that surprised others and maybe surprised yourself as well. Think about situations in which you managed to put in lots of hard work (no matter what the outcome was) and be extremely persistent. What skills did you have that allowed you to overcome all these difficult situations? What did you have inside yourself that brought you to the present day?

Now think about your independence and self-reliance—what have you done alone, without the help of others? What problems and difficult moments did you overcome all by yourself? Think about all these moments when you were alone and about all the things you achieved. Remember all these moments of strength as accurately and vividly as possible. Then you can find your strength as something that fills you; give it a visual form, a symbol.

Now, think about those things you don't know, places where you need help—compare them to all these things you hitherto have been able to deal with; compare them with your strength. Measure the sizes of these two types of situation—the ones that are behind you and the ones you are now about to face. Also think about the thing you need help with—what is it about, how would you describe in relation to what's already inside you and to what you need?

It's highly possible that the thing you need to do right now is much smaller than what you've already successfully dealt with and overcome. Your revealed weakness is not a total weakness, even though you thought so.

See the right proportions

If you do all the thought exercises above, you will have started creating your own vision of yourself, based on your experience, on what you've done so far, on your real possibilities. The stronger a self-image you create, the less important the thoughts, reactions and opinions of other people will be to you.

Your self-esteem won't be so dependent on people rolling their eyes, making grumpy faces, shouting, face-palming or sighing at you. None of these things have to lead you to the thought, "I suck." You just as well might think that your interlocutor got a sudden facial paralysis—you are the one to choose what you think. If you're building your self-worth on pretending, then you're adding value to the hallucinations and fake visions you're creating, not to yourself.

Never pretend to be someone you're not; never try to be accepted or approved of at all costs. Even if you get acceptance through your pretending, it won't help you much because then you will immediately start feeling the fear of asking yourself what will happen if the truth about the real you gets discovered. **Always look for the truth about yourself in the facts of**

your life and your past experiences, not in other people's opinions.

You don't have to fight all the time; rather, accept yourself as you already are. BUT in order to do what you eventually need to do (that is, achieve your goals), build a more reliable and real image of who you really are first. It can be difficult, because if you have a certain vision of yourself, then you also have the tendency to focus on things that suit your vision and ignore what's contrary to it. People who think, "I'm a loser" are used to diminishing the importance of the moments in life when they were successful and reinforcing the moments serving as a proof that they are losers.

You are looking at reality through the filters of your own beliefs. To start seeing yourself differently, you need to open yourself to the information you have so far been skipping. You need to give importance to the things that don't seem important to you. If you keep failing at this, you might try a few hours with a professional psychotherapist or an experienced coach who will help you start noticing these important details and seemingly small things. There's ALWAYS something to build on; you just have to consider this "something" a good foundation!

If your goal is to "be accepted" then in the majority of cases you will feel insecure, you won't know what to choose or how to behave, and your self-esteem will keep getting lower. It will also be difficult for you to "live your own life." You will be carried away by the current.

On this note, see how your goal dictates your passive attitude —wanting "to be accepted" means that someone else needs to take action, not you. In this situation, someone else decides whether you will reach your goal or not. "To be accepted" is a very poor goal to have set.

A single woman once asked me, "Is it true that there's always something to build on? Is every kind of foundation good enough? I've been building for a long time now; I graduated from a good school, then two graduate schools; I have a good job... but unfortunately, despite all this, there always comes a time when my building starts crumbling and everything collapses. I've recently noticed that what I built is only based on achievements, on having 'something' and being 'someone,' but my feelings and desires are being pushed away in this process, just like everything else I truly care about. So can I say that I don't have a good foundation? Do I keep building on sand, and that's why it keeps collapsing? I'm 36 years old, so there's lots of building material to dig in or to start rebuilding the foundations."

Everything external, everything coming from the outside is inconstant—you can have it today, but lose it tomorrow. Again, it can't be said enough—external things won't build YOUR sense of worth! If you want to be "someone," then you usually want to be this "someone" in other people's eyes—or in the eyes of a particular significant other. Admiration and social acceptance depend on tons of different factors. **The vast majority of these factors barely have anything to do with you.** Someone can throw you away not because you are not worthy or don't mean anything, but simply because it pays off for them in this particular case, or they have enough problems of their own and can't deal with anything else. Or they discharge their inner tensions onto you, the tensions caused by other people. You won't feel strong if you don't set your feelings and your own business aside.

Think whether you would like to be friends with a person who throws you away like that, a person who doesn't care about what you feel and what you desire, but instead allows the things that other people say to be more important than you. That's probably exactly how you usually treat yourself. When you are focused on being accepted by others, you keep telling yourself,

"What you feel, what you think and who you truly are don't matter! All that matters is that you finally get the prize (acceptance)!" You can't maintain healthy self-esteem treating yourself like that. You have inner strength; inner strength allowed you to get through all the previous problems in your life and got you where you are right now. The problem is that you are using it against yourself.

Some people say that they have never accomplished anything, maybe apart from many small, trivial and everyday things. That's the key to the feeling of self-worth, though: to start focusing on what already is, even if it's really small. You have to start noticing all the small good things you saw through to the end. Instead of beating yourself up over how small they are, focus on the fact that you finished them. **Start from all the small things.** Focus on what makes finishing the small things possible and on all the skills, strengths and character traits that enable you to complete all the little missions and tasks.

Here's the rub—you won't be able to see your value and strength if you keep looking in the places where they are not present! That's what you do—you say, "This is where I failed; that's when I failed, too, and oh, look at that deadline I missed four years ago! Well, here's one thing I accomplished successfully, but it's not important because it's small"

So, in other words, "Here's my strength, but let's ignore it, because it's small." Well, it's not surprising that you feel like you have no strength at all then.

Take all these small things and appreciate them; don't throw them away from your consciousness; give them a good look! These are your bricks; this is your building material—it doesn't matter if they're small. **Big structures are built of small bricks.** You've seen an acorn—it's small indeed, it fits in your hand, but it grows into something really big—an oak.

Make your own "value box"

There are many trivial things that people cannot handle. One of these things is feeling that they deserve good things in life. That's why motivational movies and books, or talks with friends where you come to conclusions like, "I can change it!," are like an inflated balloon you grab and take home. And when you are alone, you pierce it with words like, "No, it won't work" and "Other people are better," or you just frown and say, "Holy shit!," because you don't really feel you deserve more and better than what you already have.

Four hundred years ago people were burned at the stake for mockery of religion. Nowadays, the stakes are set afire when someone publicly admits to their weaknesses, when someone says she feels bad and that she could buy a one way ticket to Thailand, but it wouldn't change anything, and that she feels she's missing something all the time, because everyone is getting married and promoted and creating start-ups, while she's just going to heat up a microwave pizza in her ice cream-stained sweatpants.

The brain is very selective and, unfortunately, assigns much more importance to negative than to positive feedback, which helps in giving us the deep conviction of our low value.

That's why I think that creation of your own "value box" is so important! It can either be physical (a real box), your "confidence notebook" or a text file on your computer, but it should be **a place in which you gather all of the good things about yourself**— successes, achieved goals, situations when people said, "That won't work!," but it worked, people who have helped you even when they didn't have to, all the compliments you've heard and all the other positive small things.

Why is the "value box" so important? It helps you build your emotions on a healthy foundation and you always have something to go back to when you need to remember that you are just having a bad day today, it's not your entire life, and that no mistake of yours removes anything that you have already managed to put into the box! Then it's not just an empty repetition of "I'm valuable, I'm valuable, I'm valuable!!," but a fact-based and measurable notification, "I'm valuable, because I did this and this, so now I can also easily do that!"

Do it today!

One step at a time

Don't try to overhaul your life overnight. Just take one step at a time; that's really all you can do. My favorite example of defining a daily goal is a piece of advice a friend gave me. This friend was a career military cargo pilot, and at one time he underwent advanced survival training for the wilderness in case of being stranded in emergency circumstances. He was taught that above all, there is one thing to focus on, and one thing only: work every moment of every day to do something to improve your situation. For him that meant perhaps finding shelter or a source of water or a source of food from the land, or even simply creating a fire—he did everything he could in every circumstance to improve his situation. This is a wonderfully wise overall goal to apply to your everyday life: **work EVERY DAY to improve your situation, no matter how big or small the steps are.**

A simple yet effective way is to set simple goals for each day. The criteria for these goals should be:

1. They are realistic—overwhelming yourself with too much will only contribute to your sense of defeat if you fall short of your goal;

2. They will contribute to improving your situation in some way, shape or form;

3. They are limited—start small, and complete your tasks. Don't try to accomplish more than three essential goals a day.

You will be realizing goals that you have set for yourself on a regular basis, therefore being successful every day. Your self-esteem will be getting a daily boost from the tremendous sense of accomplishment!

A friend of mine was undergoing a difficult illness, and sometimes her goal was simply to gather the strength to go into the living room and socialize for a while with her mother. That was her daily success.

You know yourself better than anyone—do not put more pressure on yourself than you can reasonably handle. In hard times, perhaps the goal should be simply to get out of bed and get dressed and go to work and then visit the gym for 30 minutes. In good times, you might work hard on your goals for ten hours straight, then take a long hike and climb the nearest mountain. Either way, one of my primary pieces of advice in life is to listen to your body, and listen to it until you feel peace. This can translate to every form in your life! Set your goals, but also listen to your body and your mind and make the goals that bring you peace of mind within yourself. Be kind to yourself, and be gentle. Refuse to allow anger or guilt to become a daily part of your being. They are poison and can only contagiously spread, defeating all of the work that you are doing to change for the better.

Too much of anything will cause a deficiency in another area of your life, and oftentimes that is simply not acceptable. One key to maintaining your confidence is to socialize and surround yourself with people who will support your new approach to life. One idea is to sit down and create a "life list" of (1) things you currently enjoy doing, (2) things you have done in the past and would like to try again, and (3) new things you would love to learn or try. I created a bucket list of 80 goals. I've achieved some of them already, which makes me feel much better about myself and my life and gives me a lot of self-esteem. Find out what genuinely sparks your interest and then expand on that to build a new social life. For instance, if you love to read, join a book club. If you have always wanted to take a trip on a hot-air balloon, watch the Internet for promotions and opportunities, even if you go by yourself. Doing things alone is at least a little bit stressful for everyone—even for those with confidence! However, although there are many well-known benefits to socializing and going out more frequently, there is one fact that most people overlook: if you go somewhere by yourself, you are basically forcing yourself to socialize with those around you, and you do not have your friend/partner/support person there to act as your "buffer" or "safety zone." If you go to a group hot-air balloon ride by yourself, you are pretty much guaranteed to make new friends who have the same interests as you! Whether you are romantically single or not does not matter: doing activities and broadening your horizons by yourself is the key to instilling the confidence that you have been working so hard to achieve.

If you have never had high self-esteem, you may not realize that your self-development journey will have a dramatic impact on all areas of your life. Even just committing yourself to a process of change will affect your life and even add to your self-confidence and self-esteem.

Here are ten ways that your new-found self-esteem and knowledge will impact your life:

• You will ultimately be more resistant to the inevitable complications of life. This is due to the fact that you will be far less likely to admit defeat or surrender to hopelessness.

• You will be more self-confident about what you can achieve, and therefore you will be more willing to be imaginative, inventive and original. All of these qualities lead to higher rates of success and achievement, both personally and professionally. Have you ever wondered how many geniuses and prodigies this world never knew just because they never had the courage to show off?

• You will be more ambitious in every aspect of your life because you will have confidence in the fact that you can realize your objectives.

• You will have more encouraging and caring connections with others. When you have high self-esteem you tend to gravitate toward people who have the same. Those who are confident tend to attract the same type of people. Quality attracts quality.

- You will show goodness and pure class through your actions by showing others much respect, adoration and care. You will no longer see them as a danger or a threat to you. You will find that others will treat you the same in return.

- You will be more optimistic in general. You will anticipate that good things will happen.

- You will experience greatly decreased anxiety because you will become secure with your capability to cope with difficulty. You will be able to put that formerly negative brainpower into something productive and beneficial for yourself instead.

- You will be more of a risk-taker. It is a proven fact that successful people are prepared to take chances. Certainly there is the fear of failure, and certainly many people do fail. However, sometimes you just know deep within yourself that you should pursue something, come hell or high water; the journey will give you the confidence to pursue your dreams and seek out your adventures.

- You will be a much more social person. You will no longer be reluctant to meet new people or engage strangers. Every time you meet someone new they could be a new pal, business associate, client, date or maybe even your lifetime soulmate partner!

- You will be able to take criticism and use it to further develop yourself. You will be so confident that when someone says something critical it will not hurt, but will instead be helpful for self-evaluation and growth. You will be able to gauge if it is something you can use to better yourself.

Notice the frequent usage of the phrase "you will."

The word "will" is not tentative or weak, such as "could"; the word "will" is a word of faith, of determination, even of demanding that life give you more than you have received. So believe in the "will" of these ten points, not the "could" or the "should"—you WILL be a more confident person!

In German, "will" means "I want to." (The full phrase is "Ich will"—"I want to"). English and German have the same Germanic roots. Many words are interconnected. The linguistics experts point out the fact that the English word "will" comes from the German word "wollen" ("to want") and the Latin word "velle" ("wish"). In English, the word "will" is mainly used to indicate the future tense or to express inevitable events.

So... why don't you make your personal success something inevitable?

PART IV: Practical exercises and NLP tools

Congratulations! You've come to the last part of this book. We have talked about self-confidence, self-esteem, self-awareness and the important relation between these foundations. You learned that self-confidence comes mainly from real life experience and taking the right action, and that healthy self-esteem has to be consciously cultivated, actively and regularly taken care of.

Now that we have these milestones covered, it's a good time to focus on certain techniques that will enable you to boost the feeling of self-confidence and self-esteem in yourself—both temporarily and on a daily basis. These techniques will prove helpful during certain events in your life (exams, dates, job interviews, etc.), but also as an overall aid during your self-confidence- and self-esteem-building journey, as something to use every day once you attain the right mindset and have decided to proactively work on your self-confidence by gaining new experiences.

So far in this book, I have told you a couple of times either to stop or to start doing something, perceiving or thinking about something in a certain way. Now I will show you concrete examples of how exactly you can do some of these things. I will show you the mighty arsenal of tools I have used (or am still using) myself.

Neuro-linguistic programming, although it sounds intimidating and uber-scientific, is simply a fancy name for something that you actually already know: broken down, "neuro" is neurologically how your brain works; "linguistic" is language; and "programming" is simply a pattern of behavior you learn through experience. Translated, it simply means that you will be using your actions to change the way your brain processes language, and in turn your language will reflect the new way that your brain is thinking. So in essence, NLP functions in a circle; it is about directing the chain of events, thoughts, reactions, behaviors, and emotions in life, and using simple techniques to re-train your brain (mainly the subconscious) to become who and what you want to be. In the NLP cycle, how you think and what you visualize influence how you feel, which in turn influences how you react to situations.

Regarding our neurological systems, our view of the world is formed by the information we collect using all of our physical and emotional senses and intuitions.

When you learn the techniques of NLP, you will no longer be lost in a fog of emotion, unable to clearly see what is around you due to your convoluted emotional responses. Feelings and emotions fluctuate. Building solid foundations of thoughts and behaviors is the only firm basis on which to regulate the rollercoaster of your inconsistent emotions. You will see clearly, and will be mindful of your own thoughts in order to bring about the outcomes you desire.

As with any tool, it can be seen as a gift or a curse. Both self-empowering and self-defeating thoughts and visions have ways of manifesting themselves into your life's reality. There will always be outside forces that happen to you that are outside of your control. The fundamental key to NLP is not to channel positive energy from external forces to affect the direction of our lives; it is to learn how we can imbed the tools inside of ourselves in order to control our thoughts, emotions, actions and, subsequently, our reactions.

This is the beauty of neuro-linguistic programming: it gives you the tools and techniques to change how you THINK, so that you are able to change how you FEEL, so that you can change how you REACT, and henceforth alter the outcomes of your life. This tool forms the true necessary foundation upon which to build your life; although it can be used negatively, you have chosen this book because you want to make a POSITIVE difference. NLP presents techniques that are used to change our habits and our wills, and can even alter our personalities. Habits are not confined simply to our external actions; humans have just as many emotional customs as they have physical routines, and these behaviors affect the paths of our lives.

I am reminded of a story I heard a long time ago: a man is sitting on his front porch, rocking comfortably in his porch swing, talking pleasantly with his neighbor. Then they hear the telephone ring inside the house. The neighbor looks at the man and asks, "Aren't you going to go answer that?" The man wisely replies, "I own my phone. My phone does not own me."

I think often we as a society, even as humanity in general, forget the wisdom in that story: we as people own our emotions, our thoughts, our actions, our choices—they do not own us. WE are in control. We are not victims—we are the masters of ourselves, able to face the joys and sorrows that life hands us with personal ownership, and not a sense of martyrdom.

Guidelines

Before you get started, please get familiar with these guidelines:

1. The most effective way would be to proceed with the exercises in the order they are outlined in the chapter. Start with the first one, master it and then go further.
2. Don't start with another exercise until you've fully mastered the one you've already started learning.
3. Allow yourself at least three consecutive days to learn each of these exercises. Even if you think you are already fluent, don't proceed to the next one before three days. It can make you feel a little bit confused about new knowledge, especially since some of these exercises are a little bit similar to others.
4. You can either record the instructions and then listen to your voice giving you instructions, or just learn the steps by heart, making sure you understand them, and then start the exercise, with all devices (smartphones, computers, TVs, radios, etc.) off. Having your devices off is very important!
5. Before you start, make sure you will have enough time for yourself and no one will interrupt you.

6. Some of these exercises are a "quick fix" and quite easy to apply. Some will require much more effort, focus and persistence. Don't give up on them, though; they are really effective and have the ability to positively transform your subconscious in a truly amazing way.
7. All of these require visualizations skills. The better your imagination is, the better for you. If you feel that your imagination could be working better, it could be a good idea to buy a book about visualization skills or search the Internet for some exercises. I have also included three highly effective visualization exercises in my book "Emotional Intelligence Training".
8. Good luck and have fun!

Facing your inner personalities

With the help of this exercise, you will find personalities you have created in your own mind. Your mind creates personalities on a metaphorical level, present in your subconscious, and today you will meet these personalities to gather more information about them. You will realize what they are, what role they play and how they are created by your mind. Awareness of these things will help you gain distance from these personalities and many artificial roles you tend to play in your life.

These personalities are usually created to cover who or what we are really afraid that we are. Growing up, some of you surely experienced the imprinting of certain beliefs that stated that you were not good enough as you were, that you should be someone else, behave in a certain way, and so on. In social life, some of you learned and adopted the ways you "should" function, the ways you should always strive to be different than you are. Subconsciously, in reaction, we start creating many different personalities and striving to become them, as they cover these things we are afraid of about ourselves, our true nature that was always "not enough" according to society. It stops us from discovering the diamond we already are. That's why today we are going to work on removing this briar patch that has been created in our minds.

Breakdown

First of all, you have to realize the personalities you already have. People who lack confidence often tend to wear various masks and play roles to make good impressions on others and fulfill their expectations. These roles can be different; for example "a seducer," who aims to attract as many girls or guys as possible, an "expert," who wants to be perceived as a specialist in every area possible, a "cool person" who doesn't care about anything, a "party animal" who wants to have fun and drink every single night, and so on. Wearing such masks and playing such roles distracts you from feeling comfortable, as these behaviors often negate who you really are. You've probably noticed that when acting as someone you're not (for example, a person who never cares about anything), you don't feel how you'd like to feel. So now, I'd like you to give it a serious thought and to write down all the roles you feel or think you tend to play. Then, break them down into logical levels, as described by Robert D. Dilts[3].

For example, for "party animal," a description of the role could look like this:

1. Identity: Party animal.
2. Values: Having great fun, relationships with other people, being noticed by others.
3. Beliefs: *I have to dance and drink as much as possible and meet as many people as possible before I get old. I should party at least a few times a week.*

---

[3] http://www.nlpu.com/Articles/LevelsSummary.htm

4. Capability (what you do in your head when you're wearing this mask): E.g., internal dialogues such as "Life is sad when I'm not dancing drunk," "I'm afraid of being alone," "What if people stop liking me when I stop partying so often?," etc.
5. Behavior: Going to parties as often as possible, never missing an opportunity to go out, drinking a lot or taking various substances in order to be able to have more fun, constantly meeting more and more people just for the sake of meeting them, etc.
6. Environment: Bars, pubs, clubs, big events, etc.

Now, write down all your personalities, or masks, if you will, and break them down as presented above. The normal number of masks we wear is between one and three, although in some people the number is greater. For the sake of this exercise, today let's focus on no more than three personalities.

Face-to-face

The second step is to get to know your personalities in depth. That's what we are going to do now. Awareness of certain things will allow you to let some of these personalities go, and will surely allow you to gain significant distance from them and lessen your need to act out these personalities. When this desire appears, you will be conscious of it—you will know it's now on the surface.

You will also realize that you are not your personality—it's only an imprinted program that's supposed to execute certain tasks and realize certain missions.

As I mentioned earlier, all of the exercises in this chapter will be primarily about visualizations—always make sure you will have a moment of your own, so you are able to sit comfortably and allow about 20 minutes to focus on what you are doing in your head as much as possible. If the place you are staying might be too noisy to focus, you can reschedule these exercises, or play relaxing music on your headphones and ask your roommates not to disturb you for half an hour.

Once you take care of your surroundings, we can start.

Imagine a room with two comfortable armchairs. It can be a real room from your home, or some other room that you like, a room that you feel sentimental towards or a place you think is or would be really comfortable and relaxing.

Now, close your eyes and imagine you are sitting in one of these armchairs. Imagine how comfortable it is when you can sit in this armchair and just have a moment for yourself.

Now, imagine how a chosen personality enters the room. Imagine how it looks. If it's a coward, make it look so. If it's extravagant, make it look that way.

Say hello—after all, it's a part of your personality! Allow it to sit on the chair in front of you. Relax and start asking questions. It's important that you write down what you ask about and what the answer is. Don't expect very specific and concrete answers—they could be concrete, but they don't have to be. Every piece of information you get will be useful. The answers might come in the form of interrupted sentences, or what seems to nonsense—but every single answer is a clue.

If answers don't come to you quickly, wait a little bit longer. If the answer still doesn't come, just proceed to the next question for the time being and go back to the omitted ones later. Naturally, we are not contacting extraterrestrials or some kind of spiritual entities here—all the answers you get are coming from your subconscious. After every single answer make a short pause and write down what you got. Here are the questions you should ask:

1. What's the reason you exist? What's the purpose? Why do you exist in my life, in my head? Ask this question in your internal dialogue and wait for your subconscious to answer.

2. Once you have the answer, ask the next question: Since when have you existed?

3. Write down the answer and ask: What are your biggest achievements in life? What have you accomplished? How are you influencing me? What failures have you suffered? In which situations is your existence is not useful to me? What are some specific contexts in which your existence is adverse to me? Write down the answers.

4. Then ask: Do you have something I don't have? and, What would have to happen for you to let go? Make a pause and write down the answers.

5. You might have questions of your own you would like to ask. If so, great—do it now and write down the answers.

6. Take a moment to think what else you should ask about. Maybe you need a certain answer that would be important to you. If so, ask the question.

7. When you're finished, browse through the answers you have written down. See what defines this

personality, what describes it. Can you think of something that could happen to make this personality cease to exist? How are you looking at this personality now? Do you still want to keep creating it? Do you want to continue? Perhaps you would like to modify it? Have you gained distance from it?

8. Once you are done, write down your conclusions and proceed to another personality you have written down. Initiate the conversation and listen to the answers.

9. You can boldly lead longer conversations with your personalities if you like.

Once you're done working with all the personalities, you will know yourself much better. This exercise will also be of great use in your further self-development journey. It will be much easier for you to work on your beliefs and to change them now that you're distanced from them, knowing they are created by certain personalities in your head. It will be much easier for you to discern them. For example, when having a beer with friends you might come to the realization that it's now one of your artificial personalities talking to them. You will be conscious that it's now present and on top. You can then take a step back and think about what the personality wants to achieve and why it came around. The more information and data you gather, the more you understand and distance yourself from the personalities, the more you will understand how they function and hence how you function yourself.

Changing your personal history

Today we'll work on the technique of changing your personal history.

Certain events from your past can have a significant influence on how you feel now; that's why it's so important to change your perception of the past, so it's easier for you to live in the present. Success in almost everything in life is about the right perception. This exercise will help you change your beliefs and memories about all the situations in which you lacked self-confidence and self-esteem.

We often live guided by various beliefs that were born in us many years ago. So many of us still live as if they were true, apart from the fact these facts are vastly outdated and not relevant to our lives anymore. The problem is they are well-nested in our heads, which we are not often conscious of.

Thanks to this exercise, you will realize that some of these beliefs are totally useless now and truly change them, just as you would overwrite an old file with a new file in a computer. It will change your perceived timeline and will build a timeline of experiences that will support your self-confidence and self-esteem on a daily basis.

Let's begin!

1. Look for memories that could have had a significant influence on your shyness or general lack of self-confidence and self-esteem. They could be any situations that have influenced how you now feel in life. They don't have to be any big tragedy, but a context in which you think a certain memory could be affecting your present state. Take some time to recall such memories. If you can't recall anything like that—don't worry. It doesn't have to be an exact memory—it can be any situation you remember connected with a lack of self-confidence or self-esteem. Find the earliest situation you can remember in which you lacked confidence.

2. Using your imagination, recreate this situation as vividly as you can. Recall all the scents that you smelled, remember the temperature, see the colors, and hear the sounds and voices.

3. Now, with the eyes of your imagination, see yourself from an observer's perspective. Stand apart from this situation. Your point of view can be suspended

somewhere in space. See yourself in this situation and ask yourself this important question: what did you lack in that situation that held you back from feeling absolutely peaceful? What resource was it? Maybe it was certain emotions, beliefs, or knowledge about a given topic? Maybe it was something external—e.g., someone else's signs of affection? What did you need to make this situation play out like you wanted it to? If you already know, write it down. It could be a few things at once.

4. If you can't find those resources you lacked, please choose one of these: safety, love, closeness, tenderness, acceptance, understanding, trust. Just pick the one you feel describes what you think would have helped you the most in this situation. Don't take "confidence" into account, because its absence stems from the lack of one of the resources mentioned above. Pick one resource you want to work with, just one at a time for now. If you've chosen it, proceed to the next step.

5. Imagine the situation again. Now, seeing you are lacking the resource you picked in the previous step, and observing how you are behaving in this situation, exactly as you behaved originally, think about what belief was born in your head when this situation came to an end. Undoubtedly it was a limiting belief, because the situation did not play out

as you wanted. Write down this limiting belief right now.

6. Now, answer this question: have you ever had a situation in your life in which you felt you had this resource and could feel it fully, 100%? Can you remember situations in your life in which, for example, you felt full of love and were limitlessly loved? Or accepted? Find a situation in which you felt the resource with your entire mind and body. Please remember a situation in which you, even for a moment, had this resource fully. It doesn't matter how it was created, where it came from; it's only important that you knew you had this resource, you could feel it. Think of this situation and remember it as vividly and precisely as you can. Again, see the colors, smell the scents, hear the sounds, etc. Do everything you can to feel what you felt then, in exactly the same way.

7. Now, when you have this resource and you can feel it fully, think—how is it, exactly, when you feel it? How does it feel to sense it now? What kind of feeling is that? Focus on the part of your body in which you can feel it the most strongly. Where exactly is this pleasant feeling located? In your chest, in your stomach, in your head or maybe in your ears? It is big or small? A few inches or maybe several inches wide? What color, shape and physical

state does it have? Is it a gas, liquid or solid? Is it moving in a particular way? Up or down? In a spiral? Pulsating? Is it moving fast or slow? Is it light or heavy? Warm or cold?

8. Now, when you have established the specifications and location of this feeling, you have, in fact, anchored it in your body. It won't be there forever, but by recalling those parameters you will be able to bring it back whenever you wish.

9. Now that you know the feeling and you have defined and cached the feeling inside of yourself, bring back the positive situation once again and once again ask yourself what this feeling is and how exactly you feel it. Once you have it again, go back to the unfortunate memory in which you lacked this resource.

10. Imagine yourself from an observer's perspective, from the outside. Now, send this resource to yourself, in the exact visual, sensual form you created moments ago. See how the feeling nests inside of you, see how it penetrates you. See it changing your body, your look, the expression on your face and your behavior. What's now changing in this situation? Now, imagine how this situation escalates and evolves once you have obtained this resource. What has changed? How differently are you behaving—the "you" that, as the observer, you can see from the outside—what different actions are

you taking? Maybe you are making better decisions, maybe you are reacting differently to what someone is telling you, maybe you are doing something else, taking different actions or avoiding doing something. See that, right now, everything is turning out perfectly fine!

11. Once you've done this, come back to the beginning of this situation and to the first person perspective. Again, feel yourself receiving and now fully having this resource; see and feel how differently you are acting—again, repeat all the steps from the previous instruction, but now, from the first person perceptual position, from your own perspective, as yourself, feeling all these good emotions again.

12. Once you're done, think about whether there could be any other resources involved. If you feel there were some additional resources you lacked in this situation, start from the beginning, now focusing on the still-lacking resources. Go back as many times as you need to work on all the resources you lacked in that situation.

13. Now, when you have given yourself all these resources, see how this situation ends and what new belief is born in your head when the situation plays out exactly as you wanted it to.

14. Now, go through the timeline of your life and imagine a few other situations, starting from the

first situation you worked on until today. Think of all the moments you lacked self-confidence and self-esteem because you lacked these resources; think of situations that would have ended up positively had you had the resources. Also, remember a few situations in which you had the resources and how they played out when you had all you needed.

15. You can also imagine your future and see future situations in which you might lack some resources. In this case you can "go back in time," remember a situation in which you had the resources, and "send them" to your future self, using your imagination.

16. If you feel like you might need it, you can work this exercise over a few times more. If not, that's fine. If you do it with full engagement, it will hugely affect your subconscious, thus strongly supporting your present confidence.

Rebirth

This exercise will be similar to the previous one, "Change of Personal History," but we will be doing it differently.

This time, we won't be applying resources you needed in a particular situation, but will travel far back into the past, so far (before your birth) that you simply can't remember it. Obviously you don't have any memories from that period, but they're not necessary. You will imagine how it could have looked and you will see how sending yourself certain resources affects your subconscious by making a deep transformation. Open yourself to this and you will see all sorts of good things you can achieve.

We should be taught about certain laws and principles connected with thinking about ourselves from early childhood, but unfortunately, the exact opposite is constantly taking place—kids, teenagers and students are taught and re-assured that they don't know, don't have, can't do, can't achieve, etc. That's why it's hard to fully unleash our true potential.

This exercise will help you and will show you the incredible things that can happen when we actively influence our subconscious—because after this exercise, your subconscious will work as if you had been taught all these laws of good thinking about yourself in early childhood. Let's start!

1. Sit down comfortably and relax so you don't have to move. Take a deep breath and think where your future and your past are. Everyone has a timeline in their head, but we hardly ever imagine it.

Imagine it exactly how you feel it in the space around you, not logically.

1. Once you know where your past and future are, I'd like you to close your eyes and imagine that you're rising high above yourself, so you can see this timeline from a bigger perspective. It could from left to the right, bottom to top, etc. See it exactly how you feel it, in the space around you.

2. Hover above it and see it from high up, as it's leading from the past to the future. Imagine that you're now in the middle of it, right here and now.

3. Now, imagine that you're flying in the direction of your past. Starting from the point high above yourself, in your imagination, go further and further into your past. Imagine that on your timeline you can see different images from your life—maybe when you were twenty years old, eighteen years old, sixteen years old, thirteen, ten, eight, six years old, and so on. See it playing like a movie. Go even further—five years, three years—even if you can't remember anything in particular—just imagine how it might have looked. Finally you can see memories and images of yourself at the age of one year, and then a few months. Now you're right above the point where your timeline starts.

4. Now imagine that you go beyond this point and start hovering down, lower and lower, so you can

clearly see your mother with a protruding, pregnant belly. She has you inside. As a two-month-old fetus, you're just beginning to exist. Imagine this belly clearly.

5. Go inside it and see yourself as a fetus. It's really small, just starting to develop. Maybe what you see is just the initial shape of a little human being that just remotely starts to resemble a tiny infant.

6. Now, when you see yourself in the initial days of your being—reflect for a moment and ask yourself this one, very important question: If you could give an important piece of advice to yourself, now, while you're a fetus, advice that would change your life for the better, what would it be? It could be, "Smile more often," "Don't worry about what other people say about you," "Always believe in yourself," or anything else you've learned in your life through your experiences. Pick something that is true and precious to you. Once you have it, imagine yourself saying it to the fetus.

7. Imagine this advice penetrating through its skin and rooting deep inside. See as every little cell of its body starts to seep with the knowledge and understanding of what you just said. Maybe the fetus starts to move or starts to develop better as a result. See it in your imagination.

8. Now, imagine that you're the fetus. Imagine how it would feel. Imagine this knowledge getting through to you and penetrating every single cell of your body. Imagine and feel how the understanding of what you said a moment before fills you.
9. Imagine as you grow up, getting bigger and bigger; you're five months old, seven months and so on. You're growing up with this knowledge you gave to yourself– you have it in yourself; it penetrates every inch of your body.
10. You're finally being born—with this knowledge inside of you. It's a part of you and you know it.
11. Imagine that you're two years old, three years old, etc.—see how you're functioning, how you act and behave having this knowledge.
12. Imagine, as you're getting bigger and older, how you behave when you're six years old, with this knowledge rooted deeply inside of you and you fully understanding it.
13. Imagine that you're still growing; you're ten, twelve years old, and so on. You still have this knowledge deep inside of you. See different situations and imagine how you think, act and behave with this knowledge. Go further; see yourself as 15, 16 and 18 years old and so on, until you reach the stage you're at right now.

14. Now, when you're as old as you are, and you come back to your present moment, think that you feel this knowledge fully. You are this knowledge. It's still deep inside of you and no one will ever take it away. The understanding of this truth is in every single cell of your body. It's an integral part of you.
15. Now, you can also imagine your future. Think about tomorrow and about next week, a couple of weeks, a couple of months and a couple of years into the future. See all the situations that can happen when this knowledge is a part of you.
16. Open your eyes. How do you feel?
17. If you still have something important to say to yourself as a fetus, "go back in time" and do this exercise again, saying all the important things you think you should've known from the early days of your life.
18. You can repeat this exercise in the next couple days to integrate it fully into your subconscious.

The pattern of giving yourself true love

Working on natural self-confidence and healthy self-esteem starts from self-acceptance, but it doesn't end there! Self-acceptance is not enough. Self-acceptance will introduce a significant and tangible change into your life, but we aim higher! Self-love directed at your inside is much more important. It's not about arrogance, false superiority or endless self-admiration, but about authentic love that comes from the fact you like yourself and love to spend time with yourself—it comes from the belief that you're someone amazingly valuable. It gives you the sense of true warmth, self-respect and love. For some of you, it might be a novelty or something strange, but after this chapter, that will change.

Why would you not love yourself? You are a unique human being and you will spend some time on this planet. You can be your own best friend, and this exercise will help you in becoming that.

1. Take a deep breath and close your eyes.
2. I'd like you to scan through your memory and look for the best, nicest memories.
3. Find a memory about a person who had a great and positive impact on you, someone who truly loved you. It should be a person who can absolutely act as an example of someone who really loved and appreciated you. It could be anyone—maybe your grandma or grandpa, maybe your mum or dad, your son, your sister or your friend.

4. Recall a certain memory in which this person gives you their love and you can feel it in your heart.
5. Now, think about characteristics of this person. How would you describe this person? Think about the characteristics that make this person feel true love towards you. What makes this person love you?
6. Once you know what makes this person love you, imagine that you're rising above yourself and taking the perspective of this person.
7. See yourself with their eyes. Now, when you're the person who loves you, feel the love that you have for yourself. Feel its immensity. From this person's perspective, describe yourself as if you're seeing yourself standing somewhere nearby. What do you value the most in the person you see (in yourself)? Why do you love that person? Focus on the feelings you feel towards that person.
8. Now, go back to your own perspective, and feel the love coming from the person who loves you. Imagine that you're receiving this feeling in the form of some kind of energy. You can even imagine that a warm, red energy flows from that person and gets inside you. You can imagine that this energy settles in your body and you start to tangibly feel being loved. Experience these feelings. Feel how

that person perceives you and stands inside the love for you.

9. Now, think about where this feeling of being appreciated arises in your body, when you feel loved. Which part of your body comes into your mind? What does this feeling of being loved look like?

10. Think about what you feel when you start truly appreciating yourself. Think that the love you feel now, the love you received from someone else, you can pass on to someone else in turn—or to yourself, and so you start loving yourself with this love you received, the love you are overtaken by.

11. When you're totally filled with this love, imagine how it's changing your perception of your situation and of everything happening around you.

12. Now, as you feel the love and see it as, for example, a warm, red energy that's inside you, you can touch your body where you feel the energy has nested. For example, you can touch your chest, where your heart is, and feel the warmth of your body and the warmth of this love. Feel that it is right there; feel the energy; feel that you're touching it; feel its vibration; feel that you're appreciating it and appreciating yourself.

13. Once you can fully feel it, take your hand away. Every time you would like to recall this amazing

feeling of love in the future, you will be able to place your hand in the same spot and remember how much you love yourself.

14. Imagine one or two situations that will take place in the future when this deep, vibrating self-love you have will be of great use to you. This self-love is an appreciation of the greatness of all your virtues and traits, of all your value and of who you really are. Vividly visualize how these future events will play out when you have this love inside of you and you love and accept yourself 100%. To make it easier, you can place your hand on your chest, or whatever place on your body you previously chose, and imagine this warm energy that's inside you. Then see this situation with your imagination's eyes.

15. If you need some more time, make a short pause and then imagine some other situations.

16. Once you're done, relax for a while and see how differently you're now perceiving yourself. Self-perception and self-awareness are not only about describing various logical info about who you are and about your value, but also perceiving yourself through the perspective of many positive emotions such as love, kindness, tenderness, etc. All these positive emotions can push you into an incredible, positive inner transformation. You should direct all these emotions towards yourself, as they constitute

a very strong foundation for your self-esteem and self-confidence. They will also help you feel much better around other people.

17. Now, imagine yourself among other people when you have this love in yourself. See that your interactions seem totally different when you feel the self-love fully.

18. Every single time you want to strengthen this feeling of love, just remember the person who once gave it to you. Once you find that person in your head, think about the way this love emanated from them. Get into their perspective, send this energy of love to yourself, and then go back to your perspective, receive it, welcome it and accommodate it in your body. It's a beautiful feeling and when you feel loved by yourself, you can walk among people with a big, genuine smile on your face, because inside you there's something really special that gives you an enormous feeling of self-worth on a deep level.

Perceptual positions

In this exercise, we will be working with perceptual positions. It's one of the most important exercises in the process and in the entire book, so focus and engage fully. It can improve your self-esteem in a very short time. Let's do it.

1. Remember a situation in which you felt low self-confidence or you felt stressed out, a situation other people were also involved it. Don't choose a very difficult situation to begin with; choose a situation in which you felt you lacked confidence. Let's start with the situation that just came into your mind and you would like to work on. Make sure you have a piece of paper or a notebook ready.
2. Close your eyes and imagine this situation very clearly, every single detail. Recall as much as you can—what you saw, what you felt, what smells and sounds you perceived. See this situation from your own perspective, with your own eyes. Focus on your interior, on how you are reacting to this situation, what you are feeling, what you can see. Take a look around. Feel the emotions that were present during that situation. How would you describe them? What thoughts appear in your head when you're in this situation; what are you thinking about yourself and other people; what are you thinking about this situation?

3. Once you know the answers to these questions, pause your visualization and write them down.

4. Once you've them written down, go back to the visualization and imagine being in the same situation and feeling what you felt when it was taking place; then hover up, see yourself from above, and then fly to some other person; hover above them and fly into this person's head. Imagine that you're taking their perspective, becoming that person and seeing the world from their eyes. Imagine that you're that person; see their body, take a look at your hands, etc. How are you feeling right now as this person? Is it a positive or a negative state? How are you perceiving this situation? What is it to you? Are you focused more on your own problems, emotions and thoughts, or are you focusing on that other person, on yourself, standing or sitting nearby? What do you think about yourself now that you see through this other person's eyes? Do you have a negative, neutral or positive attitude toward yourself? How do you perceive this person (yourself)? Open your eyes, make a pause in the visualization and write down your conclusions.

5. Once you're done, close your eyes again and take yet another person's perspective. Repeat the same

steps from above. If there was no one else in this situation, proceed further.

6. Rise above the person whose perspective you took and become an observer. Take a look at the situation from the sidelines. Be a totally independent observer. You're not connected to any thoughts or emotions; you're looking at all this totally unattached. How are you perceiving all of this? How does this situation look to you? What are you now thinking about it? What do you think of each one of the people involved? What do you think about yourself? What kind of advice would you give to these people in this situation; what would you recommend to them? Once you have the answers, open your eyes, make a pause and write down the answers.

7. Once you've done this, close your eyes once again and now, starting from the sidelines again, fly through space and go back to your own body. Look at this situation through your own eyes and now, as yourself, notice what has changed when you look at this situation again. What has changed after this short trip around other people's perspectives? How differently do you feel and think? How differently do you think about the people who are taking part in this situation? What advice would you give to yourself and to all the other people who are there?

8. Write down all the conclusions and insights that come into your mind.
9. Once you're done—congratulations! You've just finished this exercise!

How do you feel? Probably a lot has changed in your perception of this situation. This exercise is very effective in working through thought patterns and memories, and hence strongly supports your self-esteem and self-confidence. You can now take care of future events. You can do exactly the same thing, taking the same steps. For example, you can imagine yourself in a bar or a club, meeting new people; you can imagine your job interview, your public speech and so on.

Regular practice of this exercise will allow you to gain insight into how other people might think, function and perceive reality, which will help you find relaxation and self-confidence in your body. You will also teach your mind how to function and what to expect of other people's thinking.

Later on, every time your mind enters a new context, it will naturally know how to envision other people's perceptual positions so you won't have to perform this exercise indefinitely. Do this exercise two to three times more and then, during the next couple of days, work through all of the significant events from your past and your future.

Once you do this exercise several times (up to 30), you will notice how your behavior changes when you meet other people; you will notice a change in how you instinctively feel about these situations and about yourself.

Dealing with criticism

This exercise is about creating a break between the moment of being criticized and the moment you receive and perceive the criticism. Your conscious decisions can affect the way you perceive it. This exercise is key to controlling your reactions and reacting as you want, no matter how hard the criticism is and who's making it.

Let's begin.

1. Remember a situation in which someone criticized you or said something very mean or upsetting about you.
2. Recall all your memories of the situation—smells, sounds, images, and everything about the environment. First, remember the scene

before you heard the criticism. Remember how that person looked, how you felt, everything that was around you, where you stood and where that person was, the temperature, etc.—everything, as vividly as you can.

3. Now imagine the same scenery, but there's a big, thick, transparent, bulletproof wall between you and the critic. Let it occupy the entire field of view. This wall will guard you from the criticism, prevent it from reaching you. It will give you time to consciously make your own decision about what you are going to do with the criticism, with what was said about you.

4. Now, hit "play" on your mental movie and imagine this person criticizing you. This criticism won't reach you, as you're behind the wall, but you can hear it.

5. Once you hear this criticism or mean remark, but while you still feel great as you're safe behind the wall, you can make a choice. You can just ignore it, or you can take it into account and think what lesson you can draw from it. You can disagree with it and tell the criticizing person you don't agree. You can come to the conclusion that you want to explain why this criticism is not true and start debating with this person. You can agree with it and conclude you don't want to talk to this

person anymore. You can say "no" and just walk away. You can say you will take some time to think about it and will let them know about your opinion later... and so on. Think what suits the situation the most. Who was the author of this criticism; what were the circumstances; how did they make the criticism, and what was the intention behind it? Take a moment to think about it and take your conclusions into consideration before deciding what to do in this situation.

6. Pick the option that suits you the most and when you're ready, think that by making this decision you're now making yourself ready to welcome the criticism exactly in the way you choose to. In a moment we will remove the wall and the criticism will reach you.

7. Remove the wall and use your decision to do with the criticism what you have just chosen to do. Do it now and feel this criticism integrating with your decision.

Great!

Once you have mastered this technique, you will know how to deal with every type of criticism. Do this exercise regularly when someone criticizes you; with time, your mind will get used to the fact that there's a gap between the criticism and your reaction to it in which you have time to make a decision. You can decide yourself what to do with the criticism. After an extended time of doing this exercise, your brain will re-wire and the free choice will come naturally. Voila!

Stop dwelling on bad memories

Dwelling on bad memories and unpleasant events from the past sucks. Why should you be worried now if at a certain point in the future you are probably going to forget about all these situations—most likely sooner rather than later?

But that's one of these things that are easier said than done. This technique is best used right after someone is mean to you, or when you think you messed something up. It's simple, easy and effective.

1. Close your eyes and remember a very recent time you were criticized. Bring back all that you could feel a moment before receiving this criticism. See this situation, the people, the colors, the details of the scene, etc.
2. Imagine how you felt just after receiving the criticism.

3. Remember the thoughts that appeared in your head. What were the thoughts telling you? What emotional state did they put you in?
4. Now, imagine that three hours have passed since that event. Imagine where you are and what are you doing. How are you now perceiving that past situation; how do you feel?
5. A little more time has passed and now it's the following day. To what extent are you still thinking about that situation? How much are your emotions connected to that situation? How has your thinking about it changed?
6. Now, imagine that one week has passed already. Repeat all the steps from point 5.
7. Now, repeat the same steps, but it's already one month later.
8. It's six months later. Imagine all the things again; analyze your emotions and your thinking about the past situation. Do you even think about it?
9. It's one year later. Imagine how irrelevant, silly and fuzzy that short moment from one year ago is. You have to try really, really hard to even remember anything at all from that day and that event. It's totally irrelevant now, like last winter's snow.
10. Open your eyes. How do you feel? You've probably changed your perception of this situation and your

internal representations of it. You don't feel like dwelling on this situation anymore. That's great, because as you can see, you don't need long days or weeks to stop worrying. You can start feeling significantly better here and now.

Self-confidence anchor

Anchoring is not an easy technique. Many people do it wrong and then complain that it doesn't work, but today we will establish an anchor that will work strongly and intensely in such a way that you will be able to make use of it whenever you want it.

A good anchor is established with the help of many different senses—primarily visual, but also auditory and sensory, so it's about creating a fully vivid scene that will trigger certain emotions.

Maybe some time ago you walked across the street and smelled a fragrance you used to use a long time ago. Suddenly all of your emotions and all the details of how you then lived came back to you. Or maybe you heard a song you used to listen to when you were in love with someone, and all the emotions and memories of that person suddenly came back. This natural anchor mechanism you just read about is something we can use to trigger whatever emotions we want, whenever we want.

Today we will do this with the feeling of confidence, as confidence is surely one of those feelings you'd like to have in many different situations. The first stimulus we will need for this process will be a visual cue—a particular image or symbol.

It can be an image of yourself in a particular situation or a particular place in which you are usually self-confident. If you're a good musician and you feel confident on stage, you could imagine yourself playing a great concert for a big audience, etc. However, it should be something unique, something you don't get to see every day. If this image is too obvious and common to you, then the anchor will get weaker as time passes. Maybe imagining a particular symbol will be much easier for you than imagining an entire scene, and it should be easy and effective, so you can bring it back easily and quickly in any situation.

We also need an auditory stimulus—music. Pick a song that gives you a good kick in the butt, evoking many strong emotions and feelings of strength, power and good, positive energy. This song will greatly help you trigger a state of deep and strong confidence. You can pick the soundtrack from a good movie or something by your favorite band.

Another thing we need is a concrete internal dialogue. For example: "I can do it! Self-confidence! I can deal with everything!" It should be something connected closely to the feeling and state of strong confidence, but remember that intonation and emotional message are also crucial here. Pick anything that suits you and works on you.

Rehearse it now a few times so it's said as confidently as it can be. Say it to yourself aloud, so you can actually feel it.

Finally, the third sensory stimulus—touch. You need a unique gesture, such as tapping the tips of your pointer fingers together, pinching yourself on the back of your knee, sticking two fists together—come up with something that's intense, unique and rare for you to do.

These three stimuli, launched at the same time in the same exact moment, when you're experiencing a strong emotional state, will "save" this state in more than just one part of your brain, thanks to which it will be much more effective than it would be if you just used one stimulus.

What we are going to do now will be to introduce in you a strong emotional state with the help of a vivid visualization focused on sensing and feeling as much as possible.

This exercise works best when you can listen to it on headphones and then apply the steps as you're visualizing the scene. Suggestions are given; you apply them and do everything you can to feel as much of the suggested feelings as possible, while recreating an event in which you felt confident and strong. However, it's not as easily done through written text. Hence, here are my two suggestions. First, write all the steps below enough times that you remember them clearly. This could be done with all exercises in this book, but this one is special as it involves the greatest emotional immersion and all the words used are important. When you have all of the steps learned by heart, close your eyes, play the music and do the exercise from your memory. However, it will feel harder to relax and it won't be even nearly as effective as if you actually listen to these steps and proceed as you hear the instructions.

Hence, my suggestion is that you record yourself reading these steps and giving yourself the instructions. You can use a smartphone or a computer. Don't worry about the quality of sound and the professionalism; the recording will just serve as a guideline, a road sign. First of all, we react better to our own voices; second of all, you will be 100% sure that you're doing everything right and there will be no distractions, so the immersion will be much deeper. If you're not the biggest fan of your own voice, you can ask a friend to record this for you. However, it would be best if you just did it yourself. This is a book about self-confidence, after all!

It's very important to read more and more vividly and energetically as the exercise progresses. At the peak point, you should be reading this really emotionally and sounding very excited and confident, so the "NOW!" is almost a triumphal cry. So I suggest you invest some time and energy into this exercise and take the longer way; it's totally worth it when done right. Please also remember to leave gaps so you can get into the situation, imagine certain things and focus on certain feelings.

Exactly at the moment your emotions peak and you hear "NOW!" you will pull the trigger and use all three stimuli AT THE SAME TIME (not one by one!). Thus, feeling this emotion intensely, you will establish the stimuli as the anchor. Later, when you launch these stimuli, the emotions will come back.

1. Play the song you chose so it plays throughout the exercise without stopping, looped.
2. Once it's playing, sit down and relax comfortably, but not too comfortably—don't lie down and become overly relaxed to the point that you become sleepy. Sit with your back straightened, chin slightly up, and chest protruded.
3. Think of a situation in your life in which you felt very confident, absolutely calm and relaxed. Once you pick one, imagine it. If you can't remember any particular situation, just remember the last time you felt confident—nothing heroic or extraordinary, just safe and confident. If you still can't think of anything like that, just come up with an imaginary situation. How would you look, feel and behave in this state of strong confidence? Visualize this situation you've imagined or remembered and immerse yourself into it as much as possible.
4. Focus on visual details: where you are, how it looks, what colors you see, what people are around you, what the weather's like, etc. Focus on every single aspect of this memory. Hear the sounds that were there; immerse yourself into the melodies, if you heard any. Recreate or imagine this situation as clearly and as vividly as possible.

5. Once you're there, in that situation, you can feel the small seed of confidence start to sprout. At the same time, the image you are seeing starts getting larger and much more intense. Maybe it's also becoming sharper. Maybe everything around you gets even more three-dimensional. Maybe you see that there's more action going on, or the sounds become clearer and louder.

6. Immerse yourself fully into this visualization and feel as your confidence starts sprouting more and more, infecting the cells of your body. One by one. Imagine the cells of your body getting steeped with confidence and calmness, and starting to infect other cells. Feel that now you can do anything. You don't have to be afraid of anything, because you are perfectly safe at all times. And you're an absolutely valuable person. Maybe the thought appears in your mind that all the things you were afraid of, all these limitations of yourself, were never true. They never had any importance or any meaning. They were not real at all. How would it be if from now on, forever, you stopped thinking about all these limitations and stopped believing all of these negative beliefs? Who would you be if you became this clear diamond and started feeling this immense self-trust and unconditional love for yourself?

7. Being in this situation, you start feeling this deep confidence grow more and more and more inside of you. It starts infecting even more cells in your body. More, more and more. It takes over entire organs and parts of your body. They are now filled with strong confidence and trust in yourself.

8. With the strong confidence you have in this situation, you know you can do anything; you know that you can do it, that you will make it in every situation in your life, no matter what happens. And you start feeling even better, because you now feel that this confidence fills your entire body. There's more and more and more of it. And you start feeling even better and better...

9. ... until you see that this situation brightens you with the lightness of immense confidence; now you're fully in this situation and you know it's really happening right now and you feel as this confidence grows even more, flowing through your veins and infecting every single particle of your body. Now this feeling grows inside of you and now it is inside you, fully. Now you feel that YOU ARE love, you are truthfulness and authenticity, you are honesty, YOU ARE full confidence, and you are all your healthy self-esteem, and now you feel all of this mixing into a big wave that flows through you, penetrating you

through and through. Now you know you're feeling a perfect, absolute confidence; now you know you are absolutely valuable, unique; now you're the diamond; now you feel that you can do absolutely everything, because you can deal with everything, and all of your limiting beliefs are now long gone into oblivion; now you know you are the most valuable person you are capable of creating; now you feel that this confidence grows even more and expands more and more. Now you are absolutely calm, because you feel just perfectly great. When you start feeling this confidence exploding inside of you because there's such an abundance of confidence it can't be contained inside of your body, you start penetrating through this confidence and it starts flowing from you, creating an amazing beam of light; now your entire self is this confidence; you are the confidence, confidence of the fact that you are a fantastic, amazing and valuable person, because you are ideal and perfect exactly as you are right now—**NOW!** Establish the anchor. Do it now!

10. Once you're done, open your eyes. Take a look around; relax and rest from all these positive emotions. Break the emotional state—see what's outside the window, count the lights in the room or your fingers. Take a moment to think about

something totally different and unrelated—think about what you're going to do tomorrow and the day after and what you are going to eat for lunch. Think about an interesting thing that happened yesterday.

11. Now, once you have relaxed a little bit and switched both your thoughts and your emotions to something else, go through this entire visualization once again. Gradually heat up, and once you start feeling that the confidence is exploding and flowing from you, establish the anchor again. Repeat these steps two or three times, including breaking the state (step 10).

12. Now it's time to check the anchor. Launch these three stimuli at the same time. Remember that to launch the state of confidence, you also have to empathize with the state. Stimuli help to a great degree, but you are the one consciously entering into this state; it's not automatic. The stimuli take you to the lakeside, but you have to jump into the lake. Now, launch the stimuli and re-enter the state of deep and strong confidence and fantastic self-esteem.

If you think that the anchor isn't strong enough, you can go through this process again, this time using another situation. The more vivid and stronger the situation, the better.

You can also apply this technique in everyday life—every time you do something you think you couldn't do normally, or anytime a strong emotion connected with confidence appears, use these three stimuli. For some people, it's hard to establish an anchor and trigger an emotional state artificially, so you can also do it naturally, through real life experiences. Then you can be 100% sure this anchor will work and you will have it established fully.

You can repeat this process as many times as you want and make the anchor even stronger.

You can also establish other anchors.

Enjoy and have fun!

Projection of resources into the future

Let's focus on your beliefs. We want good beliefs to become rooted in your mind even more strongly, so they become a part of your mindset and your worldview, once and for all.

To survive, though, every single belief needs certain proofs. Apart from writing down certain logical proofs to back up a certain belief (e.g., the "value box" from the previous part of the book), you also need evidence in the form of images in which this certain belief is true, or in which you make practical use of it. These will be imagined situations in which you are using these beliefs, situations that could possibly happen in the future. In the future your mind, apart from the logical evidence you have written down, will have additional proof in the form of images, which will not only make the belief more grounded, rooted and real, but will also cause so-called projection into the future. In other words, there will be an increased likelihood that if the situation really happens, you will remember this belief and it will be present in your mind.

This exercise will help you fully apply certain beliefs in specific situations through visualization of yourself giving and receiving resources for these beliefs.

Before you begin, write down all of your negative beliefs and then cross them out. Then, in the same row, write down a positive belief for each negative belief you just crossed out. Write down the exact opposites of the negative beliefs. Here's a brief example of negative beliefs people usually have: the unknown is dangerous; only a coach/therapist can help me; people will think I'm weird; I have to be special; I don't deserve love/friendship/acceptance, etc. Once you have the positive opposites for all of them, I would like you to pick a certain belief from the list.

You can instead choose a belief from the chapter "Self-confident Beliefs." Focus on the belief you most need, a belief that will help you, a belief that you believe will give you the best effects. Ask yourself, how should you think about your life, your career, your past and your future so that your belief SERVES YOU and HELPS YOU instead of bringing you down?

Remember why you already believe or want to believe in this particular belief. What proves it to be true? In your head, go through all the evidence and proof showing you this belief is real. Find them now.

What are the symptoms in your body showing you that this belief is true? Is it a particular sensation in any particular area of your body? Is it a certain emotion? If so, where is it located? Can you describe it? Maybe it's an internal dialogue saying, "Yes, that's true!" Maybe it's a symbol or a vision. How do you recognize it? Repeat this belief to yourself again and check.

Once you have the belief, concentrate on the stimulus saying it's true. Focus on the belief and try to develop it a little bit, try to cultivate the sense of genuineness of this statement, so you can feel even more that it's 100% true. Focus on it now.

Once you have focused on the belief, imagine a situation that will take place in the near future, maybe in a week, maybe in a month—a situation in which this particular belief will be of great use to you.

Imagine this situation from an observer's perspective. See yourself from the outside. As always, visualize the situation as vividly as you can—involve images, smells, sounds and all possible sensations, and once you have this situation visualized fully enough, imagine that you're sending the deep certainty of this belief into the situation that will take place soon. Imagine how it might look and sound, as you're sending this sense of certainty now and receiving it in this future situation.

Watch from the outside as this belief penetrates and infiltrates you; see how it penetrates and infiltrates you in the future. And still from the observer's perspective, see how it changes your behavior, maybe also your posture and body language, maybe your facial expressions, etc. See what you are doing while influenced by the deep certainty of this belief. See how your thinking about yourself and other people changes once you know you have this belief deeply adopted and rooted inside of yourself.

Once you've done this, come back to the beginning of this situation, and once again imagine that you're giving this belief to yourself, but this time, after having sent this belief to yourself in the future, get into the first person perceptual position and envision everything from your own point of view. Fully feel the belief, as you're receiving it, from your own perspective. Imagine as it settles and nests inside of you, until now you can feel it's 100% true. See what changes inside of you when you can feel it fully. In short, repeat exactly the same steps you took in the previous stage, when you viewed yourself from the observer's perspective.

Once you're finished and this imagined situation comes to an end, I'd like you to internally thank yourself for this belief in this situation. Say "thank you" to yourself in your thoughts; say that it's helped you greatly.

Now imagine some other situation that will occur in the near future, in which you will make great use of the same belief. Once you have it, repeat all the steps from above.

Finally, go through the same process, but with other beliefs. You will have to repeat this exercise several times, ideally during the next couple of days. These self-confident beliefs will support you internally and will allow you to act as you want to, when you want to.

Reframing the most difficult situations

Let's now work on dealing with difficult situations—the ones you're not necessarily expecting, but that can cause fear in you. The probability of their occurrence is not greater than 5%, usually smaller, but the fact alone that they possibly could happen makes many people feel scared and makes them lose their resources, even if they have worked long and hard to feel confident. The mere knowledge that a difficult situation to deal with might happen holds them back from feeling as they easily could and would like to feel.

The truth is, difficult situations can happen to anyone. Usually they don't, but even if something like that happens, you will manage it with no problem. Thanks to this exercise, you will take care of it yourself.

This exercise will help you practice many different potentially difficult scenarios, so you can go through them and do great if and when they happen in real life, because knowing the ways in which you could possibly act will diminish your fear (as you will know what exactly you can do, and how to do it).

This technique is about imagining a difficult situation and then choosing a certain behavior that will help you take it in the direction you would it like to go, so you feel good about how it plays out.

1. Imagine a difficult situation you would like to work through and practice—a situation in which you are not sure you would act like you would like to. For instance, when giving a public speech, it could be a difficult question from the audience, or forgetting what you had to say, or discovering you haven't prepared enough content, that you still have 30 minutes on stage and you don't know what to talk about. Or, when meeting new people, it could be a mean laugh or remark from someone you approached and tried to meet. Now, pick one possible situation.
2. Imagine yourself in this particular situation, from the observer's perspective, a moment before this difficult situation happens. Imagine the whole situation as vividly as you can. Hear it, smell it, sense it, touch it in your imagination.
3. Once you have done this and you are in this vision as deeply as possible, imagine that this difficult or unfortunate situation happens. Imagine a difficult question coming from the audience, someone laughing at what you say, or whatever you chose to work on.
4. Think about it and imagine this difficult situation. Once you see it and play it through, hit "pause" and

just see a static image of the situation after it has happened.

5. Now you have time to react, exactly like in the "Dealing with Criticism" exercise. How do you want to act? Find an answer? Be honest and admit that you don't know the answer to this question? Tell the audience about something else instead? Take a break? End the presentation? Maybe explain the situation? If someone just laughed when you approached them—perhaps you want to laugh back at them, walk away from them, or say something in particular? And so on. Now, choose a decision you now want to make and incorporate in your life after this difficult moment takes place. Once you choose a behavior you think is the most beneficial, imagine yourself doing it, looking at yourself from the observer's perspective.

6. Now, see other people's reactions. See how they react positively to your behavior.

7. Look at yourself again and see how good you feel, how you show positive emotions when you see that the audience or your interlocutor reacts positively. Clearly see yourself in this positive emotional state.

8. Now, rewind the situation to the very beginning, back to the moment before this difficult situation happened and look at this situation from your own point of view, from your own eyes. Imagine the

moment in which the difficult situation begins, once again, this time from your own perspective.

9. Now, hit "pause" again, think about which behavior you want to proceed with (this time it can be some other behavior or action) and apply it, imagining you are acting exactly so, right now.
10. Now, imagine how other people react positively to your action. See it from your own eyes. Focus on their facial expressions, words, and appearances; see how satisfied they are with your reaction.
11. Now, go back to focusing on yourself and about think what their reaction gives you—how do you feel once you notice it? Feel the pride coming from overcoming this difficulty; you've made it, and you won again!
12. Congratulations, you've overcome the situation, and when it happens, you won't be scared like you would have been without doing this exercise. You've changed your subconscious thinking.

Now, write down situations in which you could potentially feel afraid so you can work through all of them.

Swoosh

This is a simple technique, especially when you're already fluent with the previous ones, which doesn't consume much time and which you can practice for a few minutes every single day. Here is how to practice "SWISH," doing the steps in order:

1. Start in the now. Picture yourself in the situation you want to change: having low self-esteem. Pretend you are looking at a screen with this situation playing out on it. Pick one of the lowest points. What is going on around you? What are you doing? What do you hear and see or even smell and taste? Feel all the emotions that you felt in that situation as you watch it play out. Make the picture real.

2. Now you are going to picture yourself as a self-confident person with high self-esteem. Picture what you are doing, wearing, seeing, and feeling in this situation. Make it a perfect, beautiful, happy, wonderful scene. Feel strong, confident, joyous and content. Make it enticing and alluring to be the new you.

3. Next, take the scene of you in your worst state and make it big and colorful. Really experience how terrible you feel. In the middle of the bad scene, the

scene of the way you want to feel suddenly appears, tiny and dark. Make it as tiny as possible as if it is pulling away from you until it is a tiny dot. Then pull it back like you would a rubber band. You can feel the band get tighter and tighter.

4. Suddenly say "swoooooooooosh" while you release the rubber band and let it jump forward. The scene is suddenly in full view, big and bright. Look at it, watch it. Feel how much different you feel as the new you. Take it all in.

5. Now close both scenes entirely and focus on something else for a bit.

6. Repeat steps 1-4 five to ten times, each time swooshing/swishing faster and faster. Eventually, changing the scene from the current you to the new you should take less than a second.

7. Try looking at the starting scene that you want to change. If it is not automatically replaced by the scene of the confident you, start the process over again until the replacement is automatic.

Expectation-related pressure relief

If your friends, coworkers or family members have certain expectations of you, you have to know that these expectations don't really have much to do with you. In almost every situation other people's expectations directed towards us are usually connected to their own shortages, which they want to fulfill through another person.

Imagine that you're expecting of someone that they always keep everything perfectly clean and tidy. You rationalize these expectations by believing that everyone should take proper care of tidiness in their home. How do you know this belief is shared by the person you are directing your expectations towards? It is you who now has difficulty accepting what you define as mess, and you are projecting your belief onto the other person. If they don't clean, you can get angry. But criticism of that person doesn't say anything about that person and it says everything about you—about your beliefs and what drives you crazy. Now, that doesn't mean that you should tolerate mess and chaos and that you should accept other people's untidiness fully. This exercise is just about realizing that all of your expectations come directly from your beliefs and your own problems. It works both ways—people who have expectations of you do so because of their own shortcomings, deficiencies or beliefs.

1. What exactly do other people expect of you? Go ahead and write down the people around whom you feel you lack confidence. Then write down their expectations of you.
2. Imagine what would happen if you suddenly stopped fulfilling each person's expectations.
3. What would be their reaction? What would change in your life?
4. Once you've given these things a thought, promise yourself you will talk with these people about the expectations they have of you. Be honest with them and tell them why you might not be able or might not want to meet some of their expectations. If you are authentic and kind, you will be surprised how positively your message will be received. Also think about whether some of the expectations you perceive them to have are not actually your own expectations of yourself.

Also, try this simple visualization:

1. Close your eyes and imagine people who could or do have certain expectations of you. Imagine that there are arrows coming from their bodies to yours, almost touching you. This is a representation of their expectations of you. From some of them, there might be just one arrow pointing at you, and from others, more than one, depending on how many expectations they have of you.
5. Now, being aware of how these expectations work, you can start redirecting these arrows. Imagine that they stop pointing at you and start pointing back at the person who is sending them to you. Now, do this with every single arrow you imagined.
6. Remember your own arrows. If you have expectations of other people, aim them your own direction, so they point at yourself. This way you will recoup responsibility for your own expectations.
7. Once you've done all this, check how you feel. Freer? Lighter? Easier? Calmer?

Daily affirmations and goals (short term)

It is important to start your day off right. It is also important to make sure you stay focused. An easy way to do this is through daily affirmations. Although these steps can initially appear to be time-consuming, you can accomplish them consciously in less than five minutes every single morning.

1. Find time to focus/meditate at the beginning of your day. Find a quiet spot, even if it a common area in your residence.

2. Tell yourself five things that are positive about yourself. It takes five positives simply to undo the harmful effect of one negative statement about yourself. Also, if you haven't done it already, make the list of 35 things you love about yourself and your life. Read it every day in the morning. It's powerful. You'll see.

3. Remind yourself of your high self-esteem and confidence. Repeat affirming words to yourself out loud. For example, one powerful affirmation that I used once was, "I do not necessarily forgive right this moment, but I am open to the universe sending me forgiveness." Within two days of my beginning to repeat this affirmation, a family member approached

me to apologize for his horrid behavior from two years earlier. Coincidence? Perhaps, but the practice itself really makes you feel better psychologically. So find a positive affirmation that speaks your language and gives you a sense of peace and reinforcement, even if it is as simple as, "I am worthy of love and acceptance; I am confident in myself; I value myself, and I deserve good things in life." You can also create your own affirmations. You should feel touched emotionally by saying them out loud.

4. Tell yourself that you have control of yourself. You have the ability to do anything you want. Be cautious to prevent negative thoughts from creeping in—until you are mentally able to do this part of the exercise, speaking the affirmation out loud to yourself or writing it down daily (again, really recommended) will be a good place to begin the habit until you are ready for the next step. Anytime you win yourself over and show strong will, write it down in a text file on your computer. I mean it.

5. While you are doing this, put yourself in the mindset of being tremendously confident with high self-esteem. Feel as if you have high self-esteem. Say out loud to yourself in the mirror, while looking into your own eyes, "I am worthy of all things that are lovely and good." Do it every morning and every evening.

Present-moment awareness

Another important thing to remember is to stay in the now. Do not focus on what has happened or may happen. The past and future will only drain you; you cannot do anything about either one. Your power comes from the moment happening right now. This time, right now, is when you can change, be successful and make choices. Use present-moment awareness to help you remember this. It will also (and this is extremely powerful!) affect your prefrontal cortex—the part of your brain responsible for taking action, focusing, maintaining social intelligence and control, achieving goals and many other behaviors. Just do this exercise EVERY DAY and you will see what happens!

1. Pick the same time of day every day to do this. Pick the same peaceful place to do it in as well. Make sure no one will interrupt you. Turn your phone off. Go offline. A silent room without any electronic devices inside it should be perfect. (OK, you can keep your Kindle in the room, but put it out of sight, please.)

2. You need to have a clear and calm mind. Relax your mind and body. You can stretch a little and take a few deep breaths before you start. Your mind should become empty and emotionless. You may need to practice a bit in order to be able to reach such a state; if you're not used to silence and nothingness it can be a little difficult at the beginning. Make sure you are upright as you do not want to fall asleep. I do this exercise just sitting comfortably in my favorite chair with my back straight, looking at my piano or a blank wall in daylight. Some people do it looking at candle's flame in the dark. It's your call.

3. You want to stop thinking. You want to be able to come in full contact with reality as it is in that very moment. Thinking is a distraction. Repeat several times to yourself that you need to be fully aware of what is going on right in this moment and that you are releasing the past and future.

4. Keep your mind busy to keep it from thinking, but don't get too paranoid about thinking that you shouldn't be thinking. It will come with time—as you become better at meditating you will not have to do this so much. Turn the focus of your mind to:

    - **Listening**

Hear everything going on around you. As you become able to focus better, tune into softer sounds in the distance. Release the sounds you have just heard and focus on the present sounds.

- **Feeling**

Feel what your legs and arms are touching, how they are lying. Experience the feel of the clothes on your body. Feel the weight of your feet placed flat on the floor underneath you. Be aware of the temperatures in your environment and how your body feels sitting in a chair or standing in your current pose. Pay attention to any physical pain or discomfort. Feel negative feelings like anxiety. Pay attention to how all these feelings change as you meditate. Release from your mind what you just felt and focus on what you are presently feeling.

- **Thinking**

Pay attention to the thoughts coming and going without delving into them. Label important feelings with one word and release them. Pay attention to the new ones that come as the old ones pass. Think of it as lying in the grass and staring up at the sky. You see the clouds pass over. When the clouds go the sky is clear, just like your mind. Remember what Eastern philosophy often states: you are not your mind, you are not your thoughts. You are not your emotions. You are not sad, you are not afraid, you are not excited or depressed. Scientifically, these are just chemicals inside your brain and electrical impulses. You don't even have to continue your thoughts when they come. You are just a spectator of what's happening inside you. So observe and just let go. Emotions, feelings and thoughts come and go.

- **Breathing**

Pay attention to the shifts in your breathing patterns. They should slow as you focus on this moment. Be aware of the sensation of breathing. There are two kinds of breathing: the kind where you take a deep breath and your chest expands and your shoulders slightly rise and fall, and, alternatively, the kind where you are breathing with your lower diaphragm and it is your belly that will rise and fall, while your chest does not expand at all. This deep "belly breathing" will literally lift the burden of breathing off of your shoulders and will allow your physical awareness to go inward through breathing from your core.

If you'd like to know more about meditation techniques, I wrote a book on this topic: "Meditation for Beginners: How to Meditate (As An Ordinary Person!) to Relieve Stress, Keep Calm and be

Successful." Here's link to the Amazon store: https://tinyurl.com/IanMeditationGuide

You will also find plenty of useful mindfulness-based stress reduction tools in my free e-book which you can download here, if you haven't already: tinyurl.com/mindfulnessgift

Mirror training

Lastly, here's a simple and quick routine you can practice every single day. You don't need much time to do this, and even when your house is full, you can do it in the morning in your bathroom, before taking a shower for instance. All you need is a mirror and a few minutes of free time. Stand in front of the mirror. For an entire minute use your imagination to see movies with yourself as the main character. See your future and moments of yourself achieving success. Make these pictures vivid and colorful. In the second minute, close your eyes and think about a person who really loves you. Now open your eyes and look at yourself through this person's eyes. Feel this honest, deep love. During the entire third minute, tell yourself compliments. Talk to yourself with a strong, loud and confident inner voice. Say only nice, good things! Do this every single day; you only need three minutes a day for this effective exercise to create a change.

Now, do your best to commit these NLP tools to memory and get used to them.

Work with all of the tools I've given you. Of course, everything takes time and consistency. Ironically, you will get much more consistent when your confidence level boosts up. This is the effect I call "the upward spiral": when you improve one thing, the rest also improves. There's also "the downward spiral"—when you neglect one aspect of your life, everything around it deflates and shrinks. And the former is exactly the effect you want to have in your life: the upward spiral, gaining more and more momentum every day, building up positive emotions, actions and thoughts towards the successful life you want. And when you make it gain momentum and go really fast, at some point there's no way back.

It is very important to stay focused when using NLP. Mindfulness is key. That is the most important information to take away from these lessons: staying focused and being aware and mindful are absolutely imperative. This point cannot be over-stressed.

A way to get and stay focused is to concentrate on "NOW." What better way to stay in the now than to have a great morning routine? Starting every day with a routine centered on staying focused and reminding myself of the importance of that day makes all the difference in the world. I do not think about yesterday or tomorrow. Focusing on the day at hand is a very important part of NLP.

In the beginning of my journey, every day was another opportunity for me to build my self-esteem. I had to take time to focus every single day. It is way too easy to get distracted by other people and their priorities. Start off your day by centering your mind around yourself and what you need to do.

Outro

Congratulations! You've come to the end of this book... almost! Let's recap a little, and then I will motivate you even a little bit more!

Self-confidence comes from experience. So, DISCOVER YOURSELF and gain experience in BEING YOURSELF and living exactly as you like, or die trying! That's the only way to bring unique value to the world, the value that you ARE. And only then will you be able to say you lived your own life, not the life of a character you created. Give YOURSELF to the world. Live this life your own way! When the voice and the vision on the inside become louder and more profound than the opinions on the outside, you've mastered your life. Love yourself, be good to yourself and be the best support for yourself!

Be yourself. Why? **Because that's your only chance to attract valuable people who will be a real match for you.** When trying new things, always take small steps first, to avoid the risk of eventual failure. Always think about the worst thing that can happen and how will you handle it. And remember: be your own biggest fan. Life's too short not to.

I remember as a child, when I was in fifth grade, we all received awards for character qualities. I was such a dork that it is beyond description, but I was also very firm in my beliefs of right and wrong, and I was not afraid to stand up for them. I had just a few friends, so it was surprising to me when I received the award for leadership. I will always remember what my teacher said when issuing the award; she said, "Leadership does not always mean doing what is popular; leadership means doing what is right, even if no one else will follow." I am many decades beyond that moment, and yet when times are hard and I feel alone in my choices to take the higher, happier, but more difficult road, I remember those words. We should all realize that we are our own leaders, choose according to our best personal interests, and remember that it does not matter if anyone follows—because we have empowered ourselves and we are determined never to go back to that unhappy person we used to be.

This brings up another unfortunate but real part of life: most people have others in their lives who will essentially discourage and invalidate them, basically acting as emotional leeches. Because these are often people with whom you have close personal relationships, such as long-time friends or family members, you will experience a sincere emotional conflict when choosing whether or not to continue exposing yourself to people who can bring you down and know how to push your emotional buttons. However, the goal of this book is NOT to change others, but to reprogram our own thinking.

As a suggestion, while in the beginning stages of learning to reprogram yourself, limit your interactions with these people in your life (if they must remain in your life at all, that is). When you are stronger, more reinforced and more in control of your cycle of thoughts, actions, emotions, and reactions, then you will be better prepared to face situations that have in the past proven detrimental to you. But life is a journey, and sometimes you need to walk off the beaten path by yourself for a while in order to arrive at the destination that you truly seek.

I hope this outro chapter will encourage you to stand up for yourself and your abilities. Here's an inescapable fact: many people (possibly your friends or family!) feel insecure about themselves and want to make you feel the same way. They may be doing this on purpose; however, they may be doing it without bad intentions. They may be trying to protect you, in their own way. Some people are scared to see others succeed. It's deeply rooted in their mentality and meta-programs (the way they perceive the world—the subconscious programs controlling their thoughts and emotions).

Let me share some of my own experiences based on WHAT OTHERS SAID and WHAT I DID. I hope they can inspire you.

I love traveling. I recognize it as a positive addiction—it can boost your self-confidence beyond imagination, especially when you arrange it on your own (without a travel agency) and go alone. After my senior year at college I decided to finally take a "gap year." I had once seen some beautiful picture galleries of Morocco on the Internet and had wanted to go there ever since. My sister lives in Spain, so I decided to fly to Barcelona and hitchhike down to Morocco from there—my first solo travel outside my continent.

Everyone said I couldn't do it. Spain is known as an extremely unfriendly place for hitchhikers. I don't know why, but almost every driver looks at you as you would look at a wet dog with a lame leg, minus the compassion. The country is distinguished among hitchhikers as meriting ten out of ten "difficulty stars" when it comes to catching a ride. My sister told me she'd seen many folks sitting on curbsides with their destinations written on cardboard, totally resigned after several days of waiting. I revealed my plan to my parents as well; they told me it was a stupid plan and I should go with a tourist agency (haha!) because that's the "responsible way." My brother-in-law, a Spaniard who loves independent traveling as well and had been to Morocco before, told me I should take a bus because my travel plan was close to impossible. I spent a week in Barcelona and every time I shared my intentions with anyone, they just looked at me in that disquieting way (like, "Calm down, boy, and just get yourself a plane there, or go home and play with your toy cars"). I could have listened to all those people—because, sure, they knew their own country better than me—but I simply didn't want to. I wanted to keep the promise I had made to myself. A few days later I set out, and... it was the hardest hitchhiking of my life, indeed. I forgot to mention that at the time I didn't know any Spanish. Not a word. Maybe "gracias" and "por favor," but that was pretty much it. I had lots of adventures that first day and a few times I came close to giving up, but I kept telling myself that I would do it and visualizing myself inside a cool Moroccan truck or taking selfies in the Sahara—discarding dark thoughts and transforming them into positive energy. And I did it. I was stubborn enough in approaching and talking with people even though they couldn't speak English or said "no" (or worse) initially... and that's how I got myself a crazy ride all the way down to Morocco the very same day! I met lots of amazing people, saw extraordinary and beautiful places, spent almost two months in Africa and fulfilled one of my big dreams. Everyone told me I couldn't do it. I proved to myself I could. I'll never forget that.

Another example. Back in high school, there was this extraordinarily beautiful girl—slim, stylish, and intelligent as hell, who dressed well and moved with magical grace. She rejected all the guys who asked her out. I thought they must be doing something wrong and decided to do things my own way and take my chances. I found out the girl had interests I happened to share. I told my friends I want to asked her out and they almost killed me with laughter; they were sure there was no way a girl like that would date a pale, skinny boy like me. I wasn't sure either. She dated occasionally, but only great-looking guys: basketball players, rich and popular dudes with jacked bodies or lead singers from local rock bands. Anyway, she always looked quite bored with them. After my research I decided to hit on her. I die of stress every time I approach a strange girl. I don't know why; she's a woman, probably weaker and slower than me, but somehow it's still overwhelming. Anyway, I just DO IT, knowing I'll end up drowning in misery if I don't force myself to. Once I do, I always feel much better.

In this situation, I thought of all my successes, strengths, hobbies and basically about how cool I was to hang out with. I told myself that even though I didn't look so good I wasn't the worst—I was using NLP without even knowing about it!

I sent her a message on the Internet relating to one of her hobbies, and then, not waiting for an answer, approached her when she was sitting alone on a bench waiting for her class to start. It turned out she was really a cool, nice girl, and she liked me. First we took pictures (because she was keen on analog photography), but after five meetings we ended up in a relationship. I shut my friends up forever and had a great time.

It turned out she wasn't the love of my life but we remain good friends. I am happy I left my comfort zone and did things my own way. Now I'm sure I can meet and date a beautiful and smart girl. Otherwise I would have probably become another milksop coward guy who eventually turns into a hater of life and women. **So, listen to yourself. Don't let the social noise distract you from what you really want.**

Remember how quality attracts quality? Well, the old proverbial phrase "garbage in, garbage out" works the same way, too. Again, balance is the key. You cannot have a better social life if you feel poorly because you are not taking care of your basic, fundamental needs. Respect and take care of your body, take pride in your appearance, give your body the gift of good sleep, and stop wasting your time with superficial things such as constant television-watching and social media-checking. Sure, pick a few of your favorite things if you must, but "garbage in, garbage out"—if you are filling your head with the latest drama of who is dating whom in Hollywood or what will happen on the next season of the latest evening soap opera-type drama show, then that is time when you are NOT having fun doing something else!

It might be basic and even trite to say, but always go back to the basics: drink more water, exercise, eat better, sleep better, keep your head up (this alone makes you feel more confident), stimulate your mind with quality (read at least ten pages of a good book everyday), surround yourself with warmth and light, and if you do not like something about yourself (such as low self-esteem) then work to change it!

This is what you must do if you want to get ahead: **COMPLETELY CUT OFF EVERYTHING THAT DOESN'T SUPPORT YOU.**

Start with the basics, retrain your brain and patiently watch, wait, and observe yourself slowly growing into the person you know you truly are and truly want to be! If you are at a job and have been eyeing a promotion, then start dressing more professionally and asking for more mentoring from those above you.

When you're walking down the street, hold your back straight, with your chest pushed forward. Hold your head up, with your chin slightly upwards, and look straight. Keep your arms close to your body (unless you want to look like a douchebag), but take bigger steps. Be relaxed and take your steps firmly. That's more than enough to tell others, "I'm self-confident" using your body language—and to tell your own brain the same. Yes, I have to say it—sometimes you have to fake it until you make it! Do it as long as it takes to make it your habit. The mere fact of walking like that will trigger the emotion of self-confidence in you. Moreover, other people will see you as a calm, decisive and strong person.

Did you know that a smile (even a fake smile) makes you feel better even if you are sad? That's a good example of anchoring—think about it. The smile is already connected with good emotions in your brain. The same goes for other simple things, like body language. Try to observe confident people, such as actors, rock stars and millionaire businessmen and then simply start to move and dress a little bit more like them. Don't be afraid—modeling successful people's behaviors (noticing what works for them and what they never do) doesn't mean you are not yourself anymore. Just get your own distinctive style inspired by successful people and learn from the best, without trying to be or clone them. Freely play with life and open yourself to new, different possibilities. **DARE! You MAKE your life what you want it to be**, and in the process you will feel empowered to continue on with pursuing your path.

And let us not forget about that rut we can all so easily fall into in life. We do the same things, we see the same people, and we do not often allow ourselves to step outside our comfort zone! It is just easier that way, I understand, but it is also the best way to keep your life stagnant and boring. Make "Go places and do things!" one of your new mottos! Yes, keep up with the routines of positive reinforcement discussed in this book, but also give yourself permission to try new and interesting things! Although it sounds contradictory, scheduling time for spontaneity and fun is good for you! It will fill that need for balance that is so necessary to a happy, fulfilling life.

We all have our rituals. You go to the movies only with one of your friends, you do groceries and other shopping only in certain shops, and on Wednesdays you allow yourself to eat your favorite pasta. It's perfectly normal. But anytime something new comes, something that interferes with your routine (e.g., a chance to dance with a beautiful lady, a call from a handsome devil who wants to take you for a date, or a job offer in Barcelona) you could miss the opportunity by acting out of fear that someone will destroy the order that you've built. Regularly ask yourself what it is that you're expecting in a given moment of your life.

Start changing your habits: eat something different for breakfast, drive to your office by another route, and go to lunch at a Japanese instead of Italian restaurant. And so on. Throw away phrases like, "I always drink coffee in this cafeteria," "I usually buy Japanese cars," "I only buy used clothes," etc. Those habits addict you and attach you to a narrow definition of yourself, giving you a predetermined label. Try new things!

Meditate daily and utilize whatever means you have at your disposal to make the techniques work for you. Here are some ideas: keep a small daily diary notebook; draw a chart or diagram of your goals and break them down into categories; paint or draw a picture; or even record yourself talking to yourself about your goals and dreams, kind of like verbal journaling. Different people have different learning methods, and you can find the one that best works for you. I keep a diary. Education, such as this book, should be approximately 20% of your journey, but the remaining 80% comes from ACTION. With the help of this transformative process, you can get a bright and exciting vision of what your life could really, truly be! Your dreams are within your grasp!

Remember, once you have started your journey towards change, the only things that separate those who succeed and those who do not are perseverance and determination. DO NOT QUIT. Be patient, for it is a journey, but never, ever give up. You may fall, but you must stand back up every time, brush yourself off, learn a lesson, take notes and keep going—it is the only way to win! **That, and that alone, is how you find the real strength and confidence that we all so greatly deserve: by committing to a process and sticking to it!**

Allow me to share this final story: at my high school graduation, as tradition dictates, our principal (a seemingly grumpy, ex-military, curmudgeonly old man) started out his address to the graduating seniors. Of course, he started by saying how he searched high and low through books from the greatest philosophers of our time for the best words of wisdom to share with us as we began our adult lives.

Certainly, by this time I was rolling my eyes and thinking, "Oh, this is going to be soooo boring." But then, he continued by saying, "...and I found what I was looking for in the most unexpected of places: *Winnie the Pooh's Little Book of Wisdom*." I was at first shocked, then thrilled as he read us his favorite passages. Therefore, I will do the same. Using the unsurpassed wisdom of Winnie the Pooh, remember that just as Christopher Robin says to Pooh:

"If ever there is a tomorrow when we're not together, there is something you must always remember. You are braver than you believe, stronger than you seem, and smarter than you think." - A.A. Milne

One last thing before you go—can I ask you a favor? I need your help! **If you like this book, could you please share your experience on Amazon and write an honest review (http://tinyurl.com/ReviewConfidenceBook)?**

It will take just a minute of your time (I will be happy even with one sentence!), but would be a GREAT help for me. Since I'm not a well-established author and I don't have powerful people and big publishing companies supporting me, I read every single review and jump with joy like a little kid every time my readers comment on my books and give

<u>me their honest feedback!</u> **If I was able to inspire you in any way, please let me know!** It will also help me get my books in front of more people looking for new ideas and useful knowledge.

If you did not enjoy the book or had a problem with it, please don't hesitate to contact me at <u>contact@mindfulnessforsuccess.com</u> and tell me how I can improve it to provide more value and more knowledge to my readers. I'm constantly working on my books to make them better and more helpful. Thank you and good luck! I believe in you and I wish you all the best on your new journey!

Your friend,

Ian

My Free Gift to You – <u>Get One of My Audiobooks For Free!</u>

If you've never created an account on Audible (the biggest audiobook store in the world), **you can claim one free** audiobook **of mine**!

It's a simple process:

1. Pick one of my audiobooks on Audible:

http://www.audible.com/search?advsearchKeywords=Ian+Tuhovsky

**Shortened link:
http://tinyurl.com/IanTuhovskyAudiobooks**

2. Once you choose a book and open its detail page, click the orange button "Free with 30-Day Trial Membership."

3. Follow the instructions to create your account and download your first free audiobook.

Note that you are NOT obligated to continue after your free trial expires. You can cancel your free trial easily anytime, and you won't be charged at all.

Also, if you haven't downloaded your free book already:

Discover How to Get Rid of Stress & Anxiety and Reach Inner Peace in 20 Days or Less!

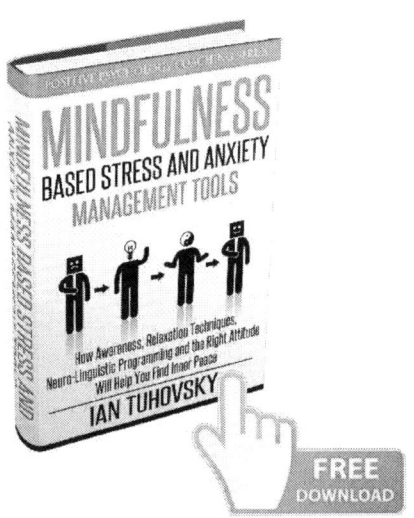

To help speed up your personal transformation, I have prepared a special gift for you!

Download my full, 120 page e-book "Mindfulness Based Stress and Anxiety Management Tools" for free by clicking here.

Link:

tinyurl.com/mindfulnessgift

Hey there like-minded friends, let's get connected!

Don't hesitate to visit:

-My Blog: www.mindfulnessforsuccess.com

-My Facebook fanpage:
https://www.facebook.com/mindfulnessforsuccess

-My Instagram profile:
https://instagram.com/mindfulnessforsuccess

-My Amazon profile: amazon.com/author/iantuhovsky

Recommended Reading for You:

If you are interested in Self-Development, NLP, Psychology, Social Dynamics, PR, Soft Skills and related topics, you might be interested in previewing or downloading my other books:

Paperback version of "Confidence: Your Practical Training" on Createspace:
https://tinyurl.com/IanConfidencePaperback

->Emotional Intelligence: A Practical Guide to Making Friends with Your Emotions and Raising Your EQ

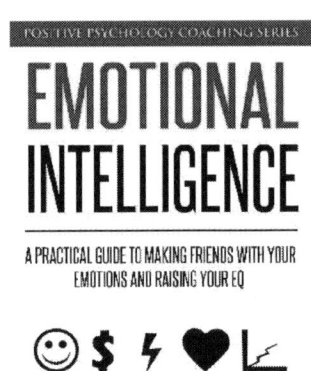

Do you believe your life would be healthier, happier and even better, if you had more practical strategies to regulate your own emotions?

Most people agree with that.

Or, more importantly:

Do you believe you'd be healthier and happier if everyone who you live with had the strategies to regulate their emotions?

...Right?

The truth is not too many people actually realize what EQ is really all about and what causes its popularity to grow constantly.

Scientific research conducted by many American and European universities prove that the **"common" intelligence responses account for less than 20% of our life achievements and successes, while the other over 80% depends on emotional intelligence.** To put it roughly: **either you are emotionally intelligent, or you're doomed to mediocrity, at best.**

As opposed to the popular image, emotionally intelligent people are not the ones who react impulsively and spontaneously, or who act lively and fiery in all types of social environments.

Emotionally intelligent people are open to new experiences, can show feelings adequate to the situation, either good or bad, and find it easy to socialize with other people and establish new contacts. They handle stress well, say "no" easily, realistically assess the achievements of themselves or others and are not afraid of constructive criticism and taking calculated risks. **They are the people of success.** Unfortunately, this perfect model of an emotionally intelligent person is extremely rare in our modern times.

Sadly, nowadays, **the amount of emotional problems in the world is increasing at an alarming rate.** We are getting richer, but less and less happy. Depression, suicide, relationship breakdowns, loneliness of choice, fear of closeness, addictions—this is clear evidence that we are getting increasingly worse when it comes to dealing with our emotions.

Emotional intelligence is a SKILL, and can be learned through constant practice and training, just like riding a bike or swimming!

This book is stuffed with lots of effective exercises, helpful info and practical ideas.

Every chapter covers different areas of emotional intelligence and shows you, **step by step**, what exactly you can do to **develop your EQ** and become the **better version of yourself**.

I will show you how freeing yourself from the domination of left-sided brain thinking can contribute to your inner transformation—**the emotional revolution that will help you redefine who you are and what you really want from life!**

In This Book I'll Show You:

• What Is Emotional Intelligence and What Does EQ Consist of?
• How to **Observe and Express** Your Emotions
• How to **Release Negative Emotions** and **Empower the Positive Ones**
• How to Deal with Your **Internal Dialogues**
• How to **Deal with the Past**
• **How to Forgive** Yourself and How to Forgive Others
• How to Free Yourself from **Other People's Opinions and Judgments**
• What Are "Submodalities" and How Exactly You Can Use Them to **Empower Yourself** and **Get Rid of Stress**
• The Nine Things You Need to **Stop Doing to Yourself**

- How to Examine Your Thoughts
- **Internal Conflicts** Troubleshooting Technique
- The Lost Art of Asking Yourself the Right Questions and **Discovering Your True Self!**
- How to Create Rich Visualizations
- LOTS of practical exercises from the mighty arsenal of psychology, family therapy, NLP etc.
- **And many, many more!**

Direct Buy Link:
https://tinyurl.com/IanEQTrainingKindle

Paperback version on Createspace:
https://tinyurl.com/ianEQpaperback

->Communication Skills Training: A Practical Guide to Improving Your Social Intelligence, Presentation, Persuasion and Public Speaking

Do You Know How To Communicate With People Effectively, Avoid Conflicts and Get What You Want From Life?

...It's not only about what you say, but also about WHEN, WHY and HOW you say it.

Do The Things You Usually Say Help You, Or Maybe Hold You Back?

Have you ever considered **how many times you intuitively felt that maybe you lost something important or crucial, simply because you unwittingly said or did something, which put somebody off?** Maybe it was a misfortunate word, bad formulation, inappropriate joke, forgotten name, huge misinterpretation, awkward conversation or a strange tone of your voice?
Maybe you assumed that you knew exactly what a particular concept meant for another person and you stopped asking questions?
Maybe you could not listen carefully or could not stay silent for a moment? **How many times have you wanted to achieve something, negotiate better terms, or ask for a promotion and failed miserably?**

It's time to put that to an end with the help of this book.

Lack of communication skills is exactly what ruins most peoples' lives.
If you don't know how to communicate properly, you are going to have problems both in your intimate and family relationships.

You are going to be ineffective in work and business situations. It's going to be troublesome managing employees or getting what you want from your boss or your clients on a daily basis. Overall, **effective communication is like an engine oil which makes**

your life run smoothly, getting you wherever you want to be. There are very few areas in life in which you can succeed in the long run without this crucial skill.

What Will You Learn With This Book?

-What Are The **Most Common Communication Obstacles** Between People And How To Avoid Them
-How To Express Anger And Avoid Conflicts
-What Are **The Most 8 Important Questions You Should Ask Yourself** If You Want To Be An Effective Communicator?
-**5 Most Basic and Crucial** Conversational Fixes
-How To Deal With Difficult and Toxic People
-Phrases to **Purge from Your Dictionary** (And What to Substitute Them With)
-The Subtle Art of **Giving and Receiving Feedback**
-Rapport, the **Art of Excellent Communication**
-How to Use Metaphors to **Communicate Better** And **Connect With People**
-What Metaprograms and Meta Models Are and How Exactly To Make Use of Them To **Become A Polished Communicator**
-How To Read Faces and **How to Effectively Predict Future Behaviors**
-How to Finally Start **Remembering Names**
-How to Have a Great Public Presentation
-How To Create Your Own **Unique Personality** in Business (and Everyday Life)
-Effective Networking

Direct link to Amazon Kindle Store:

https://tinyurl.com/IanCommSkillsKindle

Paperback version on Createspace:

http://tinyurl.com/iancommunicationpaperback

-> Meditation for Beginners: How to Meditate (as an Ordinary Person!) to Relieve Stress and Be Successful

Meditation doesn't have to be about crystals, hypnotic folk music and incense sticks!

Forget about sitting in unnatural and uncomfortable positions while going, "Ommmmm...." It is not necessarily a club full of yoga masters, Shaolin monks, hippies and new-agers.

It is a super useful and universal practice which can improve your overall brain performance and happiness. When meditating, you take a step back from actively thinking your thoughts, and instead see them for what they are. The reason why meditation is helpful in reducing stress and attaining peace is that it gives your over-active consciousness a break.

Just like your body needs it, your mind does too!

I give you the gift of peace that I was able to attain through present moment awareness.

Direct link to Amazon Kindle Store:

https://tinyurl.com/IanMeditationGuide

Paperback version on Createspace:
http://tinyurl.com/ianmeditationpaperback

->Zen: Beginner's Guide: Happy, Peaceful and Focused Lifestyle for Everyone

Contrary to popular belief, Zen is not a discipline reserved for monks practicing Kung Fu. Although there is some truth to this idea, Zen is a practice that is applicable, useful and pragmatic for anyone to study regardless of what religion you follow (or don't follow).

Zen is the practice of studying your subconscious and **seeing your true nature.**

The purpose of this work is to show you how to apply and utilize the teachings and essence of Zen in everyday life in the Western society. I'm not really an "absolute truth seeker" unworldly type of person—I just believe in practical plans and blueprints that actually help in living a better life. Of course I will tell you about the origin of Zen and the traditional ways of practicing it, but I will also show you my side of things, my personal point of view and translation of many Zen truths into a more "contemporary" and practical language.

It is a "modern Zen lifestyle" type of book.

What You Will Read About:

• Where Did Zen Come from? - A short history and explanation of Zen
• What Does Zen Teach? - The major teachings and precepts of Zen
• Various Zen meditation techniques that are applicable and practical for everyone!
• The Benefits of a Zen Lifestyle
• What Zen Buddhism is NOT?
• How to Slow Down and Start Enjoying Your Life
• How to Accept Everything and Lose Nothing
• Why Being Alone Can Be Beneficial
• Why Pleasure Is NOT Happiness
• Six Ways to Practically Let Go
• How to De-clutter Your Life and Live Simply
• "Mindfulness on Steroids"
• How to Take Care of Your Awareness and Focus
• Where to Start and How to Practice Zen as a Regular Person
• And many other interesting concepts…

I invite you to take this journey into the peaceful world of Zen Buddhism with me today!

Direct link to Amazon Kindle Store:

https://tinyurl.com/IanZenGuide

Paperback version on Createspace:

http://tinyurl.com/ianzenpaperback

-> [Buddhism: Beginner's Guide: Bring Peace and Happiness to Your Everyday Life](#)

Buddhism is one of the most practical and simple belief systems on this planet, and it has greatly helped me on my way to become a better person in every aspect possible. In this book I will show you what happened and how it was.

No matter if you are totally green when it comes to Buddha's teachings or maybe you have already heard something about them— this book will help you systematize your knowledge and will inspire you to learn more and to take steps to make your life positively better!

I invite you to take this beautiful journey into the graceful and meaningful world of Buddhism with me today!

Direct link to Amazon Kindle Store:
https://tinyurl.com/IanBuddhismGuide
Paperback version on Createspace:
http://tinyurl.com/ianbuddhismpaperback

About The Author

Author's Blog: www.mindfulnessforsuccess.com

Amazon Author Page:

http://www.amazon.com/author/iantuhovsky/

Hi! I'm Ian…

. . . and I am interested in life. I am in the study of having an awesome and passionate life, which I believe is within the reach of practically everyone. I'm not a mentor or a guru. I'm just a guy who always knew there was more than we are told. I managed to turn my life around from way below my expectations to a really satisfying one, and now I want to share this fascinating journey with you so that you can do it, too.

I was born and raised somewhere in Eastern Europe, where Polar Bears eat people on the streets, we munch on snow instead of ice cream and there's only vodka instead of tap water, but since I make a living out of several different businesses, I move to a new country every couple of months. I also work as an HR consultant for various European companies.

I love self-development, traveling, recording music and providing value by helping others. I passionately read and write about social psychology, sociology, NLP, meditation, mindfulness, eastern philosophy, emotional intelligence, time management, communication skills and all of the topics related to conscious self-development and being the most awesome version of yourself.

Breathe. Relax. Feel that you're alive and smile. And never hesitate to contact me!

Printed in Great Britain
by Amazon